Quo Vaditis

Quo Vaditis

The State Churches of Northern Europe

edited by John Broadhurst

Gracewing.

First published in 1996

Gracewing
Fowler Wright Books
2 Southern Ave, Leominster
Herefordshire HR6 0QF

UK ISBN 0 85244 382 X

Typesetting by Action Typesetting Ltd,
Gloucester, GL1 1SP

Printed by Cromwell Press
Broughton Gifford, Wiltshire, SN12 8PH

Contents

Quo Vaditis

John Broadhurst

Tradition has it that St. Peter fleeing from Rome at the time of the persecution of Nero met the ascended Lord coming into the city and asked him *'Domine quo vadis?'* (Lord, where are you going?) and Christ replied 'I am coming to be crucified again'. Peter took this to mean that he was going to suffer for him a second time. So he turned and re-entered the city where he met his martyrdom. The question 'Where are you going?' is one that Christians frequently need to ask themselves. Are they going to their God-given destiny, or are they pleasing themselves? Do they serve Christ or personal whim? It is a question which applies to Christians both individually and collectively.

This series of essays written by traditionalist members of the State churches of Northern Europe seeks to ask this question of those Churches. To understand the full implications of our present situation we need to understand where we are coming from and see our destiny in relation to our origins. The Churches of Scandinavia and England have a very dissimilar history yet they were forged in the turmoil of Reformation Europe. In many ways they are similar, each seeing themselves as the ancient Catholic Church of their nation, possessing much familiar to the pre-Reformation period including episcopacy and the sacramental system.

There is a deep-seated problem underlying European theology and geography. Until recently, to be born in Scandinavia was to be a Lutheran, to be born in England an Anglican, to be born in North Holland a Calvinist. The implication of this basic fact is that these religious systems have no claim of themselves except their establishment in a particular geographic region. Those who live within the region are formed by a religious system which finds itself in power through the accident of history. Truth cannot be the preserve of random geographical chance. Almost from the outset, Scandinavian Lutherans and English Anglicans have been troubled by the nonsense of their isolation and the inconsistency inherent in their claim to be Catholic Churches. Catholicism cannot exist in isolation and the purely local is the antithesis of the catholic. The impulse for the Ecumenical Movement largely came from these quarters, and, particularly in matters of Faith and Order, has continued to be sustained from Anglican and Lutheran sources.

In the period following the First World War all these churches have suffered a major decline, both in influence and numbers, and increased secularisation and liberal theology have done much to erode the original perceptions of the Church. The contributors of this book nearly all come from this National Church Tradition. Underlying the thesis that the present difficulties are problems of established churches there is an inconsistency. The problems commonly found in these churches can be attributed to their separation, isolation and historical legal establishment. However I am certain that readers from other countries in Churches that are not established will rapidly identify with many of these problems and most of the analysis in this book. This begs a basic question. What is it that makes these churches, and those unestablished churches that originate from them, different from Rome and Orthodoxy? At the Reformation different monarchs sponsored different reformers and moulded the Church in the image set out by their client. The monarch did not take the national church and make it Lutheran or Anglican. He took from the universal Church the right to regulate and decide on doctrinal and other matters, usurping that right to himself. That he sponsored Lutheran, or Calvinist, or Anglican Reform is incidental. This is highlighted in the United Kingdom where the Crown sponsors Anglicanism in England and Presbyterianism in Scotland: the alternative system being at first persecuted and later disadvantaged in the other parts of the same nation.

Henry VIII called himself Supreme Head of the Church of England and since the time of Elizabeth I monarchs have been called Supreme Governor. The first title is thought offensive because it ultimately usurps the position of Christ Himself but many think the second title perfectly acceptable. However, a Governor is a regulator. What the monarch, and therefore the State, is asserting is that the faith, order and practice of the local church will be decided by them without any necessary reference either to the universal Church, or indeed to Scripture.

The effect of this separation in England can be clearly illustrated by some simple facts. Before the Reformation all parish churches were dominated by large rood screens with a crucifix and pictures of the saints as the focus of the building. After the Reformation these were removed and the Royal Coat of Arms put in their place.[1] The impact must have been quite devastating for the worshippers and the message quite clear. The King was in charge. Thomas à Becket had been the most popular English saint, but now to possess his picture or a book about him was punishable by death. Becket had defied a previous king in the name of the universal Church.

Only recently the previously private oath taken by every diocesan Bishop has been published. It makes disturbing reading.

> 'I ... do hereby declare that your Majesty is the only Supreme Governor of this your realm in spiritual and ecclesiastical things as well as in temporal and that no foreign prelate or potentate has any jurisdiction within this realm and I acknowledge that I hold the said bishopric as well the spiritualities as the temporalities thereof only of your Majesty...'[2]

The denial of papal and other foreign power is historically understandable, as is the assertion that the monarch is the possessor of the temporalities of the Church. The State is the guardian and ultimately the possessor of all property of every religious and secular group. What is neither understandable nor defensible is the assertion that the spiritualities are the possession of the State. Sometimes it is asserted that this refers to properties and revenues. This cannot be so as this is precisely what the temporalities are. It refers to the spiritual character of the Church and its belief. It is difficult to understand how generations of diocesan Bishops have taken this oath without protest, even though some have privately expressed difficulty with its wording.

It could be thought to be little more than a quaint and interesting remnant of a past age but recent events demonstrate that this is not so. In a case in the High Court of Justice the Revd. Paul Williamson summonsed the Archbishops of Canterbury and York, together with the Church Commissioners, arguing that it was invalid for the Church to legislate in a way contrary to the Elizabethan settlement and the Coronation Oath. The question is whether there is anything 'given' in the Church of England. The Judgement against Fr. Williamson is probably the most Erastian ever made in a Court.

> 'An established religion is subject to state control as regards doctrine, government and discipline.'[3]
> 'The Church of England is established by law in England. The doctrine of the supremacy of Parliament means that Parliament may on its own legislate for the Church.... According to established principles and in the eyes of English law, the change objected to, whether or not a change in doctrine and however fundamental, was validly effected.'[4]

In other words absolutely nothing is given and Parliament may in principle do exactly what it wills with the Church. No liberal has protested about this judgement or even seemed to notice its implications.

Much is made in the modern church about the issue of disestablishment which has been on the English agenda for more than 150 years and is a very popular theme in contemporary Scandinavia. Bishop Colin Buchanan in his recent book 'Cutting the Connection'[5] sets out fully the history and the implications of the English Establishment. He makes much of the liberation that disestablishment would bring to the Church of England. Interestingly his book does little to address the issue of doctrine. Who decides what the Church believes, what it practises and how it lives? By what right does the local Church exist in isolation, or indeed act as if it were the universal Church? Disestablishment is an irrelevance unless this prior question is faced. Erastianism is a serious problem for members of state Churches but theological myopia is a more serious problem for all separated Churches.

In most situations established Churches are relatively static and therefore the Establishment could be seen as an influence retaining the remnants of the universal tradition. It is only in recent years in countries such as Norway and Sweden that the State has sought to affect doctrinal and moral norms. Many of the founding fathers of the Catholic Revival in the Church of England were seriously concerned about demands for restoration of the Convocations and disestablishment. They saw that this could compound the problem of separation and isolation. It solves nothing for the local church to seize for itself that which the State has stolen from the universal Church. Disestablishment can only possibly serve Catholicism and Truth if the leadership of the local church is formed in the universal tradition and committed to a process of convergence with the rest of the universal Church. Otherwise the idiosyncratic life of the local church becomes progressively less Catholic and ultimately less recognisably Christian.

Writing as we do from within an 'Established Tradition' we recognise that nearly everything that we have to say is reflected directly in sister Anglican and Lutheran Churches throughout the world. In many ways the problems that we face are compounded rather than simplified by the independence and self-regulation of those Churches. We remain utterly committed to the restoration of the universal in the lives of our local churches.

In modern theology the model of 'communion' has recently become the most popular model for the Church. Theologically communion (*Koinonia*) is the expression of that perfect unity which exists between Christ and his Church. Each Christian by Baptism becomes a partaker in the mystery of God and participates in the perfect communion of the Holy Trinity. That relationship puts upon the Christian the constraints of Faith, Hope and Love. The New Testament gives the vision of a people united in purpose because of their unity with Christ. If Christians are to be faithful to the Lord it can only be expressed in their struggle to be, and remain, one family united in faith and love.

St Paul tells us that we see 'through a glass darkly' (1 Cor.

13.12). In other words our perception of the truths of God, and our communion with Him, is obscured by our frail humanity and our continuing sinfulness. In this world we are not yet what we are to be in God's purpose. He exhorts the early Christians to be faithful to their calling using a multitude of metaphors to enforce the relationship. 'You are the Body of Christ and individually members of it' (1 Cor. 12.27) asserting the truth that the Christian Faith is essentially communal in character. Each and every image of the Church is essentially a corporate image. People of God, the new Israel, the Kingdom, the Vine, the Flock, and many others are all essentially communal pictures. The New Testament imperative is that Jesus died and rose for *us*, therefore he died and rose for *me*. It is only with the rise of the Anabaptists and other radical reformers that we find a reversal of this imagery. Personal faith to the exclusion of communal belief, or as a first principle, is a distortion of the Gospel. 'Christ died for me' is a post Reformation picture, and as a statement of first principle, or of faith, it is a denial of the collective and corporate impulse that runs through the Old and New Testaments. 'None of us lives to himself and none of us dies to himself' (Rom. 14.7). 'If one member suffers all suffer together' (1 Cor. 12.26).

This Anabaptist distortion has in varying degrees affected all the churches of the Reformation leading to a Church which places undue emphasis upon the value of personal belief and interpretation. One man's belief is of its very nature another man's heresy. We have indeed come a long way from Paul's conversion when Jesus says 'Saul, why are you persecuting ME?', enforcing the essential unity between Christ and the Church. A real and inescapable tension consequently exists in all the Churches of the Reformation between individual and local perceptions on one hand (Protestantism at its worst) and the corporate claims of universal tradition on the other hand (Catholicism at its best). Those Christians who seek to assert the universal and biblical inevitably find themselves hampered by the fact that in their Churches such a belief is portrayed as just 'another point of view'. Nothing is absolute and no point of view can have any ultimate ascendancy. The Church of England oscillates between Catholicism, Evangelicalism and Liberalism. Aidan Nichols analyses these three traditions and concludes 'Anglicanism is so very much three churches within one that no satisfactory ecumenical negotiations can ultimately be carried out with it (not, at any rate to the point of organic reunion).'[6] The Lutheran Churches have a similar trio of Classical Lutheranism, Pietism and Liberalism. Members of each group are subjected to an endless round of frustration as mutually contradictory perceptions gain the ascendancy and then wane in rotation. Ecumenical schemes with Catholics and reformed churches progress and then collapse. The recent history of the Church of England is littered with failed unity schemes. In the situation which exists in the national Churches nothing is absolute, and ultimately nothing is TRUE!

In the Acts of the Apostles we find the early Church sorting out its first major crisis at the Council of Jerusalem. When the Church is later established in the Empire this system continues with Constantine and his successors sponsoring universal Councils and enforcing their decisions. It is significant that Nestorians and Monophysites existed at the fringe of the Empire or beyond its borders. In a real sense the Empire became a tool of the catholicity of the Church. After its collapse the Church continued in its conciliar mode, a strengthened Papacy replacing the role of the Emperor in the West. Though it would be simplistic to present this as a golden age, it is not difficult to identify the main stream of Christianity throughout this period, or to find its central doctrines and practices.

The rise of the nation state in the western world gave rise to a host of tensions which led to the break up of the previous international/catholic Christendom. Religious and national wars led to a Europe with several mutually exclusive Christian systems and a real confusion as to the nature of truth. *Cuius regio, eius religio* is a frequently asserted Reformation dictum. It is factually true, but quite devastating in its implications. We are what we are because of a series of historical events. What is true or false does not enter into the picture! Each nation is formed in a particular interpretation of the Christian faith by an historical accident. For Anglicans the Councils of the undivided Church are true only in so far as they are in accord with the word of God: 'They may err, and sometimes have erred'.[7] In other words they are not, in themselves, or of themselves, true at all.

However, Anglicanism and Lutheranism both saw their Churches as a part of the universal Church and eventually settled down as static national Churches with an agreed, and sometimes rigorously enforced, set of beliefs and practices. Within traditions quite wide divergences exist: Anglicanism in Ireland is very different in history, theology and ethos, from its sister Church in Scotland. In a similar way Lutheranism in Denmark is quite different from that in Sweden. In each state the national Church developed its own ethos and practice. Traditionalists through the ages have always stressed the universal against the purely local, and each Church has found itself living with the tension between the faith of the undivided Church and its own confessional statements. The historic statements established at the Reformation have given a settled basis under which these conflicting views can co-exist. In each of these Churches the inner core of the tradition was conserved with the scriptures and the creeds, allied with an agreed (and usually Episcopal) structure of ministry. The power of the state was used to maintain this balance and keep in unity the different groups in the Church.

What has changed? Firstly the later development of the Enlightenment has developed the role of the individual to such a degree that an exaggerated respect for personal freedom and opinion has become the mark of a civilised society. Society, responsibility, duty, and even family have all become old fashioned and outmoded concepts. This has affected every strand of our lives and now threatens the Church. Religious anarchy and antinomianism now reign supreme!

The establishment of the Church, which once held it close to the old universal tradition, has now become an instrument of oppression seeking to enforce the views of an increasingly secular world upon the believers. In Scandinavia secular authority has promoted women priests in one place, homosexual marriage in another, and Christians have found themselves unable to oppose these innovations. In England the Church has liberalised apace and establishment effectively means that its members have no recourse to the law of the land. For all members of Established Churches the secular establishment of the Church is a Babylonian captivity of enormous proportions. The Church defends every view except traditional Christianity.

Justice exists for every group *except* orthodox Christians within the National Church.

How should orthodox Christians respond? They are no longer in unity with the majority in their national Churches, rejecting their interpretation of the truth. Many of their assertions are taken to be falsehoods. The Faith of the apostolic Church, and any notion of revealed truth, find themselves in an extremely hostile environment. Contemporary perception has replaced Revelation and Reception. Many of the actions and teachings of the national churches are contrary to the tradition of the early Church and have the effect of driving traditionalists to the fringes of the Church they have loved. There is an irony in the fact that they are the most unhappy of people. They suffer at the hands of the Church, yet for them the Church is both an instrument of the Kingdom and a part of Christ's plan for the salvation of mankind. How are they to survive in a community which is at times faithless, at other times apostate, and acts in a way that often deliberately excludes orthodox belief and practice?

Notes

1. Eamon Duffy, *The Stripping of the Altars* (Yale University Press, 1992), p.485.
2. Colin Buchanan, *Cut the Connection* (Darton Longman Todd, London, 1994), p.84.
3. *Rev. Paul S. Williamson versus The Archbishop of Canterbury, The Archbishop of York and The Church Commissioners* (HMSO, London, 1994), p.7 lines 11–12.
4. op. cit., p.7 lines 21–23 and p.8 lines 10–11.
5. Buchanan, op. cit.
6. Aidan Nichols, *The Panther and the Hind* (T & T Clark, Edinburgh, 1993), p.177.
7. *Articles of Religion* ('Thirty-nine Articles'), Article XXI.

Anglicanism and the death of the Anglican Mind

Samuel Edwards

As a prevailing feature in the life of the Anglican churches, the Anglican mind is all but dead. This is analysis, not epitaph; a description of reality, not a prescription for despair. In fact, it may well prove that wrapped within this gloomy shroud there is reason for orthodox Anglicans to hope.

The Anglican mind fell victim to a degenerative, parasitic disorder, which itself is now in the process of dissolution, having all but consumed the institutional host which sustained it. The culprit parasite is Anglicanism.

The Anglican mind (also referred to as the Anglican Way or the Anglican ethos) was a variety within the species of the Christian mind. To be sure, there was a distinct flavour to its mixture of aesthetic, moral, and intellectual styles – a sort of golden moderation, reflecting a blend of the temperaments of the British, Celtic, and Norse cultures which were a part of the making of England, yet there was never any serious contention that such things as distinguished the Anglican mind from, say, the Roman or Gallican or Iberian or Germanic or Slavic or Greek or Syrian or African or Oriental Christian mind were indicative of a difference in kind. All these were at least implicitly considered to be local or cultural streams flowing from the great well of Christian orthodoxy, and the Anglican mind habitually enriched and renewed itself by drinking liberally from all of them.

The Anglican mind, in its highest state of development, was supple without being flaccid, liberal yet disciplined, conservative yet open. It recognised that the opposite of protestant is not catholic, but corrupt, and that the opposite of catholic is not protestant, but sectarian. Even at its most polemical, it sought more reconciliation with its opponents than triumph over them. In every generation of its life – from Hooker and Field to Taylor and Cosin to Wesley and Wilberforce to Keble and Pusey to William Temple and Michael Ramsey – it has produced pastors and theologians who exemplify these characteristics. Its ethos informed an entire family of national Churches. Now, however, though the Anglican intellectual tradition remains alive in certain individuals and groups of Anglicans, it can no longer claim to have any substantial influence on what currently passes for life in the national and international institutions of the increasingly moribund Anglican Communion.

It should be noted that the death of the Anglican mind in the institutional Anglican Churches is not an isolated phenomenon or a curious, rather sad sideshow. Rather, it is a subset of the moribundity of the Western Christian mind which lies beneath the continuing slow decay of western civilisation and thought. This, too, is the result of a parasitic infestation, in which the parasites are the various ideologies – the '-isms' – which foolishly pluck up one flower from the garden of reality and seek to make it the focus of the entire garden at the expense of all the other flowers, forgetting that the separation of the plant from that in and by which it has been rooted and grounded – Reality Himself – ensures both the death of the plant and the marring of the garden.

It is necessary to spend some time considering the characteristics and consequences of -isms in general, so that at length we can see what has happened to the Anglican mind in particular at the hand of Anglicanism. An '-ism', as the term is used here, is an ideology. It is an intentionally comprehensive system of belief which attempts to interpret and organise reality in accordance with a single idea or agenda. This idea or agenda it substitutes for God or religious dogma.

Please note that this definition refers to an '-ism' as a system of *belief*, not a system of *thought*. This is quite deliberate, for -isms actually have the effect of inhibiting thought. Indeed, they end (and often begin) by substituting slogans for thought. This is one of the things that makes them so attractive to fallen man, who is lazy and likes nothing better than a chance to appear to be intelligent without the effort of actually exercising his intellect. Thought – logical analysis and intellectual synthesis – is the deadly enemy of -isms, and this accounts for the mania among ideologues for politically-correct ways of expression, for the purpose of these is to bind and direct thinking into channels which do not threaten the credibility (and thereby the existence) of the ideology. Since the ideologue does not believe in concrete, objective truth, he lacks the conviction of the orthodox Christian that the truth will eventually triumph (with our assistance or without it), and therefore he must exercise himself to guarantee the success of his -ism by whatever means.

It might be argued that all -isms derive from or through Nominalism, which (in consequence of its rejection both of the notion of a common nature and its focus on God as absolute Will rather than absolute Being) laid the foundation for the collapse of Christendom into the abyss of individualism, relativism, and positivism. After all, the road is open to the complete dissolution of thought once one accepts such nominalistic propositions as that which asserts that the classification of things into categories is a matter of subjective decision on the part of, and for the convenience of, the taxonomist, rather than a recognition on his part of an objective, inherent, natural commonality which existed prior to the classification.

As has been mentioned already, -isms are parasitic in nature. This is unsurprising. Error is always a parasite on the truth; were it not for the element of truth in the error, the error would have no existence at all. An -ism often behaves in much the same way as does a creature known as a rhizocephalan, or 'roothead'. This relative of the barnacle attaches itself to a crab, pierces the crab's shell, and injects specialised cells into the crab. These quickly subvert the crab's immune system so that it can no longer recognise the roothead as an intruder rather than a part of itself. They then take over the crab's internal systems, shut down those which they do not need (including, interestingly enough, the generative organs) and convert the crab into nothing more than a factory for the production and support of more rootheads. The net result is the destruction, if not of the crab's life, at least of its basic purpose (the production of more crabs) in the interest of the production of more rootheads.[1]

The ultimate result of an -ism, in the intellectual, moral, and aesthetic as well as in the biological sphere, is the destruction of the very thing upon which it centres its attention. It erects an idol, but (so to speak) it then loves it to death. Theologically speaking, -isms are forms of idolatry, for, whether explicitly or implicitly, they uniformly put something less than God in the place of God.

As the result of idolatry is always the eventual humiliation, or even the destruction, of the idolaters (and often of the larger group of which they are a part), so is the result of the -ism. Thus, on the political scene, ideological liberalism destroys liberty and after anarchy (which can never be tolerated for long) it ends in tyranny. Likewise, ideological pacifism paves the way for war; militarism destroys the military; nationalism brings down nations (and imperialism empires); feminism destroys women. Rationalism destroys reason, issuing in madness; activism overwhelms measured and purposeful activity, resulting in *accidie*; sentimentalism jades the affections, precipitating anaesthesia.

In the history of the Church we see the same phenomenon amply demonstrated. For example, Calvinism and Lutheranism brought about the dissolution of the Reformed and Evangelical vision of a renewed and more faithful Church, and Protestantism as a whole, by accepting the false characterisation of itself as anti- catholic, and thus paved the way for the overthrow of the Reformation by the French *philosophes* and the German liberals. In each case, a shift of focus within the institutional manifestations of these movements away from the original vision, of their founding figures and toward narrower aspects of that original vision led eventually to a failure of the movement to achieve its goals, and to the emergence of a new and permanent denomination existing either in truce or in competition with the parent Church – a result quite contrary to the intent of the founders to reform the existing Church.

The Anglican Church, on its face, probably had less reason to succumb to emergent denominationalism than the continental Churches, having gone out of its way to avoid claiming that it was more than part of the true Church of Jesus Christ. Yet by the middle of the nineteenth century, the denominational style of self- consciousness had taken firm root in it and the

erosion of the Anglican mind at the hands of Anglicanism had
already begun.

It is noteworthy that the very word, 'Anglicanism', (according to the *Oxford English Dictionary*) has no recorded written
instances prior to 1846. In the same way that consciousness
precedes speech, phenomena tend to predate the words which
designate them, but not by much. So it is safe to assume that the
erosion of the Anglican Church's concept of itself as the
reformed Catholic Church in England into an assumption that it
was but one of a variety of denominational options began before
1846, but not by very much. The roots of the shift are likely to
be found in the situation of the Church following the Revolution
of 1688, when a general weariness with religious strife found
expression in a broadening tolerance for, and enfranchisement
of, non-Anglican Protestants, which was eventually extended to
Roman Catholics and non-Christians in the nineteenth century.

This attitude of tolerance need not have been, but nonethe-
less was anti-ecclesiological, which contributed substantially
to the theological tepidity which characterised the following
century. The association (fairly or not) of the High Church
party with the Jacobite cause seriously impaired their ability
to mount an effective challenge. As it was, most of the opposition to the decline in the self-concept of the Established
Church was instinctive rather than reflective, which made it an
easy mark for charges that it was mere Tory prejudice. The
High Church party indeed vigorously opposed such reform
through the 1830s, and the Oxford Movement itself was occasioned by a reform measure, but in fact (as by this time was
being more clearly articulated) their opposition was not based
on an undifferentiated hatred of change but on the reasoned
conviction that if the Church of England was what her formularies said she was, a Parliament which now included many
who had nothing in her should not be dictating reform to her.

It was the misfortune of the Oxford Movement that it
arose when secularising liberalism had attained a well-nigh irre-
sistible momentum. The nineteenth century was the first full
century in the age of -isms, and the intellectual land-
scape of the time, both ecclesiastical and secular, was cluttered
with them. The list of them would be good fodder for a Gilbert
and Sullivan patter-song: Liberalism, Socialism, Communism,

Fascism, Conservatism, Romanticism, Impressionism, Scientism, Fideism, Anglo-catholicism, Anglo-papalism, Evangelicalism, Ritualism, Ultramontanism, Unitarianism, Universalism, Humanism, Feminism, and so on almost *ad infinitum* and certainly *ad nauseam*. In such a climate of fragmentation, it is hardly surprising that the genuinely comprehensive and unifying vision of the Body of Christ toward which the Oxford Fathers (continuing in the central stream of the Anglican Way) were pointing would not have sustained success in effecting and maintaining the full interior renewal of the Anglican Churches.

Given that historical environment, it may have been practically unavoidable that the Tractarian movement would decline into Tractarianism and become just one among a variety of rarely co-operating and frequently competing ideologies within the Anglican stall of the fold. Combined with the tendency to confuse the God- given order of the Church with the humanly-constructed institutions that are meant to serve that order, the lesser heirs of the Catholic renewal (with some shining exceptions) led the movement into the status of one party among many, with interests to be balanced against those of the others (the same thing happened on the Evangelical side). For the health of the Anglican mind, this was not a good thing. The initial character of the renewal movements was prophetic, but (again with notable exceptions) they became political, and serious thought about the long-range implications of ideas and policies is not a normal component of the politician's makeup.

As the Anglican mind was supplanted by Anglicanism, and in exact proportion to that pre-emption, the institutional Anglican Church began to be excessively concerned with questions of its identity. 'What does it mean to be an Anglican?' and 'how is Anglicanism distinctive?' became new and fashionable questions, asked in scores of different ways with scores of different answers. This sort of concern is a salient characteristic of any organisation which has been infested by an -ism. It results from the loss of a true focus on the central purpose for which the institution exists, which is a consequence of the '-ismatic' substitution of internally-focused, institutional concerns. The loss of the original purpose issues in the loss of a sense of identity, and since the human person is so constructed that he cannot bear such chaos, he is likely to accept any plausible alternate purpose that is proposed.

Another key symptom of infestation by an -ism is a preoccupation on the part of the infested institution with its own survival, and this is certainly evident in the multiple reports and schemes documenting and suggesting means of combating the numerical decline of the various Anglican Churches in the First World. This concern implies the existence of an unspoken assumption that the institution is intended to continue its independent existence indefinitely. So far as the Anglican Churches are concerned, this is a clear sign of a major shift in self-understanding, since the Anglican Reformers never intended or envisioned that the institutional separation within the Church would continue indefinitely, still less that it would come to be considered an acceptable state of affairs. They would have found fatuous and bizarre in the extreme the notion that a national Church could unilaterally alter basic elements of the common ecclesiastical order without both destroying its internal relations and fatally compromising the prospects of restoring its impaired external relations. Yet such is the very attitude now firmly rooted in the centres of governance and learning in the First World Anglican Churches.

Anglicanism insinuated itself by slow degrees and with little notice on the Anglican Church, which was to become its host. Like the rhizocephalan mentioned earlier, once in place inside, it began to take over the organism, to anaesthetise its defences by undermining the Anglican mind, and to subvert its purpose from the fostering of Christians to the making of denominationalist Anglicans. At the latter task, it has proved all too effective. The capacity of the institutional Anglican Churches in the First World to accomplish their designed purpose has practically vanished on all but the parochial level (and even there it is all too rare). The prospect that the parasite will soon have destroyed its host is very real. In the judgment of some, this has already happened in principle.

Yet, for a people formed by the Resurrection, the virtual death of the Anglican mind and the dissolution of the ecclesiastical institutions commandeered by Anglicanism is not an unmitigatedly bad prospect. After all, taken both as persons and as a whole, Anglicans are not crabs. The dissolution of institutional structures may leave us naked for a while, but it will not of necessity be fatal. The Anglican mind may no longer have an effective life in the institutional Anglican Church, but that is bad news more for the institution than for its members. In what setting these dry bones may live is as yet an open question. Whether they shall live is not, and we may confidently hope that at the breath of the Holy Spirit, they shall be knit together, clothed in power, and spring up an exceedingly great host which will move resolutely forward in faith.

Notes

1. Those wishing to learn more details about rhizocephalans will find them in an article by Dr. Stephen Jay Gould of Harvard University entitled 'Triumph of the Root-Heads', published in the January 1996 issue of *Natural History*. I am indebted to the Reverend James Johnson of Dodge City, Kansas, for bringing this article to my attention.

The Collapse of the Reformation: A perspective on the Lutheran Tradition

Bernt Oftestad

During recent decades the great European state Churches have faced deep crises over decreasing membership and theological and spiritual conflicts. These crises are not bound to any specific confession, but vary in accordance with the confessional framework. Deeply affected by this process are, however, the Protestant state Churches, especially the Church of England and the Lutheran state Churches in Scandinavia and Germany. All of them derive from the Reformation their spiritual character, their confessions, their structure and, last but not least, the state Church system.

The establishment of the secular power as the governor of the Church was a consequence of the Reformation. This arrangement, representing a dramatic break with tradition, is in different ways still present in the Anglican and Lutheran state Churches to this day, perhaps most overtly in Scandinavia, especially in Denmark and Norway. But at the same time the monarch of the sixteenth century, personally responsible for the religious life of his subjects, and therefore the Head of the Church, has been replaced by the secular, modern State, which has radically changed the arrangement.

But the Church cannot co-operate with a modern State without losing her spiritual identity. Authorities in the state Churches have gradually changed doctrine and liturgy in order to reflect the political and cultural agenda of the secular society. Protesting movements within the Churches have been suppressed. Only a minority of clergy and lay people try to stand up against this process. Many others realise the situation is fatal, but have lost their courage. We could interpret this as a moral disaster consequent on defeatism, but the situation must be considered in a more analytical way. Do we today face a spiritual and cultural situation which amounts to the ending of the Protestant story? Did even the Reformation itself in the last analysis collapse, with the Reformation Churches as early as the sixteenth century bearing within themselves the embryo of today's disaster?

I

The Reformation is a spiritual and political process with different aspects and phases. Some will underline the personal element, for example Martin Luther's spiritual experience as a monk and his fight against the clerical authorities. Others will stress the cultural situation in Europe and look at the Reformation as a part of a wider process towards a more personal religion. In discussing such theories, it is easy to forget the fundamental historical issue involved in talking about a Reformation at all. This concept was not created by Luther or his colleagues, who by no means intended to start a reformation. The decisive event which created the idea of a Reformation was the Roman Catholic Council of Trent, which took a stand on behalf of the Church on the theological problems which Luther and other theologians had taken up and tried to solve. Most of the theological themes taken up by Luther were burning questions in late mediaeval theology. The decrees and canons of the Council decisively split the western Church, but at the same time they made it possible to interpret the preceding process of theological conflicts as a special epoch in the history of the Church, definable as 'Reformation', and in this way they contributed to the transformation of the Protestant movement into confessional churches. The Reformation was not a reformation in the sense of creating new churches, but it was a theological and spiritual conflict within the late mediaeval western Church, which resulted in a breakdown of her spiritual unity.[1]

The Roman Catholic identity of the Lutheran reformers is evident from their behaviour and their writings. Luther himself, like many of his friends, was a Roman Catholic priest, although he rejected the Roman Catholic doctrine of ordination and priesthood (the Lutheran Reformation did not ordain anyone for service in its communities until 1535).[2] Throughout his life Luther expressed his fidelity to the creeds of the old Church, because of their coherence with Scripture, and he emphasised the sacramental unity, because of the one baptism, between the Reformation movement and the Roman Catholics. Luther's friend, Philip Melanchthon, who was a great Reformation theologian and a humanist as well, tried during his entire life to re-establish a doctrinal consensus between the conflicting parties, based on the creeds of the ecumenical Councils.[3] But the Roman Catholic identity and obligation of the Lutherans is most authoritatively expressed in their fundamental doctrinal document of 1530, the Augsburg Confession. The Lutheran representatives at the Diet of Augsburg claimed that the doctrine in their confession was based on Scripture and on genuinely Roman Catholic tradition. In the Augsburg Confession loyalty to the old creeds is clearly emphasised: the Lutherans did not uphold heresies already condemned by the Church, and they tried to justify their own doctrine from Scripture, the ecumenical creeds and the Fathers.

The Augsburg Confession must be regarded as a Roman Catholic confession, and the people behind it considered themselves to be genuine Catholic Christians. They had not spoiled the unity of the Church: they were not Donatists, either theologically or in practice. The only 'crime' they had committed, was the elimination of certain abuses, which had found their way illegally into the Church. They asked to be respected as faithful members of the Church, and they only claimed the right to diverge from the official ecclesial view over questions regulated by human law. They realised the conflict with the episcopate on this issue, but the bishops had to be tolerant and large-minded, if they intended to save the unity of the Church. The unity was ultimately sacramental and based on doctrinal consensus among the communities, and the main task of the episcopate was to protect and encourage this unity. A great problem in Germany was that most of the bishops were princes as well, and they might be tempted to establish an external unity in the Church by means of political pressure and violence. The traditional Roman Catholic ecclesiology did not prevent such a process; therefore the Lutherans propounded their doctrine of the 'Two Kingdoms', to deal with these problems of order and unity. They took it for granted that the Church would have an episcopal structure, but at the same time they took a strong stand against any episcopal tyranny based on secular power.[4]

For modern liberal Protestants the Roman Catholic identity of the reformers is an inconvenient fact. When they encounter it, in Luther for example, they regard it as a psychologically understandable reminiscence of his Roman Catholic past. When they observe the Catholic aspect of the Augsburg Confession, they tend to characterise it as a consequence of political pragmatism, necessary if the Lutherans were to avoid persecution from the imperial authorities for heresy, since the Empire was ideologically founded on the Catholic doctrine of God. Liberal Protestantism interprets the Reformation by means of a 'hermeneutic of suspicion'. But the positive ideological aim of the liberal Protestants is to detect the effect of the emancipating 'gospel' in history, and they regard the Reformation as a decisive breakthrough of such an emancipation, because of its critique of mediaeval theology and piety. We must therefore understand its substance in accordance with the 'gospel', the rational and emancipating structure of the historical process. The 'gospel' is in the end the rational substance of history.

This modern and liberal concept is conditioned too much by ideological interests. Historically, the Reformation does not represent such a deep and epoch-making break from mediaeval traditions and institutions. The real collapse of the mediaeval pattern of thought and the political and religious systems of the Middle Ages began as early as the thirteenth and fourteenth centuries, when Occamism and Nominalism, conciliarism and a new piety among lay people developed and left the old mediaeval philosophical and religious systems behind. Luther as well as Calvin was deeply inspired by the old theological tradition, and especially by Augustine.

Luther's political views, and his hermeneutic principles as well, are more rooted in the early Middle Ages than in his own contemporary period. The reformers do not represent any anticipation of the Enlightenment or of modernity.[5]

II

The small reformation communities which grew up just after 1520 could not avoid conflict with the Roman Catholic episcopate. Luther and the reformers had to face a jurisdictional problem, and they tried to devise different provisional solutions. The relationship to the episcopate was naturally a serious problem during the Diet of Augsburg in 1530. But the negotiations at Augsburg did not solve any problems. The Roman Catholic theologians could not accept the Lutheran doctrine and practice, and the Augsburg Confession was rejected by the Emperor. The only possible outcome was a war between the two opposing religious parties, which eventually broke out sixteen years later. Not until 1555 was a practicable solution to the confessional problem in Germany found. The Diet of Augsburg in 1555 suspended the question of confessional truth, in order to give the Protestant princes equal rights with the Roman Catholic princes within the Empire. Although the sentence *cuius regio, eius religio* is not found in the official documents of 1555, it expresses the practical consequence of this solution. The foundations were laid for a pluralistic solution to the European confessional problem. But could it be regarded as a genuine ecclesiastical answer, in accordance with authentic theological principles? The confessional basis for the Protestants was first of all the Augsburg Confession, but the political solution of 1555 not only suspended the question of doctrinal truth as such, but even the original context of the doctrinal question, which according to the Augsburg Confession was the Roman Catholic Church.[6] The Lutheran communities' religious freedom was not only protected by Protestant princes, but were governed by them as quasi-bishops as well.

Luther wanted to revive the ministry of *episcope* from the old Church. What the Church required were bishops eager to build up her spiritual life and to protect her against heresy and devastating religious processes. During the 1520s the Reformation communities were already experiencing a pressing need for a such an *episcope*, since only a few of the Roman Catholic bishops had joined the Reformation. If the new communities were to have any kind of episcopal structure, it would have to be established on a new foundation. Luther and his friends felt they had no authority to put it into effect, but they asked the Elector of Saxony for help, who called together a group of men to visit the reformed communities. In this way the ministry of the superintendent was institutionally established and the structure of the later Lutheran state Church was founded. The young Reformation movement in Germany needed an ecclesiastical superstructure, and the only possible way to get it was to co-operate with the prince. He was a pre-eminent member of the Church and therefore responsible not only for the spiritual life of the congregations, but for religious conditions in his land as well. Although Luther regarded it as an emergency measure in a dangerous situation, this provisional solution turned out to be a permanent arrangement, which established the pattern for the later process of reformation in Germany and Scandinavia.[7] The Reformation in Denmark and Norway was carried out by the king just after his military victory in a civil war. Especially in Norway, where the Roman Catholic Church was intact until 1537, the Reformation was 'imported' by secular authorities using military power.[8]

With the reformation by kings and princes a new Protestant system was set up. The monarch assumed the right to govern the Church as a quasi-bishop, and his subjects were compelled to accept the Protestant religion of the monarch; nobody had any right of dissent. The only solution for dissenters was to leave the country, though later they did establish themselves in some free areas. The ancient ideal of religious unity within a given society was perpetuated in the new nation States. This process placed the Reformation movement in a new context, decisive for the interpretation of its main theological causes: justification by faith alone and the principle of scriptural authority.

III

The Lutheran state Churches are all born of the Reformation. This kind of Church presented a totally new political, ideological and legal context for the original reforming message of Luther and the other reformers. As early as the Renaissance and the Reformation the contours of the modern State had become apparent. During the period of absolutism this state system emerges as the most attractive one for the European politicians and their rulers. But absolutism drastically changes the Church's situation. Her government is from now on a prerogative of the royal majesty. The ruler is, however, bound to the traditional confession of his country; nevertheless, this religious obligation is not a consequence of his membership in the Church, but an aspect of his power as monarch. The integrity of the local congregation is suspended and the right of vocation is from now on administered by the king and his cabinet. Ordination administered by the bishop is the only sign of the spiritual integrity of the Church. The Lutherans who traditionally had a positive and, in some respects, a servile attitude towards the secular powers did not realise that absolutism was a threat to the Church. On the contrary, the Lutheran clergy in Denmark and Norway supported the introduction of the absolutist state system, since it gave them social prestige and greater authority.[9]

The modern liberal democracy, established in the Scandinavian countries during the nineteenth century, is usually regarded as a revolutionary break with the former absolutism. The old privileges of the nobility were abolished, and equality before the law, and freedom of speech and religion, were introduced. The people won the right to govern themselves through their elected representatives. A civil sphere of discussion and debate, where public opinion could be influenced and formed, was established. As far as such socio-cultural and political changes were concerned the modern democracy was a revolutionary break with absolutism. But democracy did not nullify the modern State which had been introduced during the seventeenth century. On the contrary, the democratic State is a modern State, liberal in its administration and governed by law.

The ideal of equality, liberty and fraternity, inherited from the French Revolution, was the guiding star for the Scandinavian social democracy of our own century. This political movement, which has dominated the political life in Scandinavia in recent decades, created the politically active state and the modern social welfare state, blotting out the classical difference between the State and the civil society, which was typical of the traditional democracies of the nineteenth century.

Freedom of religious faith was one of the democratic liberties established in the nineteenth century, and democracy consequently stimulated the development of religious pluralism in society, trying to abolish all aspects of religious coercion on the part of the State. The nineteenth century was dominated by this process of emancipation. But the state religion and the state Church, originating from the Reformation and confirmed by the absolute monarch, were not abolished. The consequence of this strange synthesis of evolution and status quo was a State which displayed two different images. Traditionally, the State was confessional, but the introduction of the democratic system produced the liberal State. Such a State with such an ambiguous nature had the right to govern the Church.[10] The effects were in the long run fateful for her spiritual life and her integrity. It is not possible here to analyse all the large and small incidents which demonstrate the nature of this political and spiritual process. Instead we will concentrate on its fundamental structure.

The content of Christian preaching is a historically transmitted truth given in Scripture and the confessions. The Church, which is entrusted with apostolic truth and which transmits it in kerygma and dogma, has an organisation which is not only human in nature, but which is also legally founded in the *ius divinum*. Last, but not least, the Church preaches and guides her members in issues concerning the individual and social life in society and the family in accordance with moral ideals derived from Scripture. The modern liberal democracy has in principle a relativistic and pragmatic view on questions of truth, rightness and morality. According to democratic ideology, free, rational and public discussion will produce what people will accept as binding on their everyday life, because in order for any law to be passed, it has to be acceptable to the majority of the people. Therefore the real aim of public discussion is to produce the (theoretically rational) majority opinion.[11] Although democratic theory holds that the opinion of the majority is in principle rational (if the majority is enlightened), at the same time it has to admit that prevailing official truths and concepts must be regarded as historically and socio-culturally conditioned. The modern democracy is in the end ideologically based on relativism. But in spite of this relativism, it is a dogma of the democratic ideology that a more complete understanding of reality and consequently a better world are located in the future, especially via scientific progress. Relativism is, in other words, to be combined with a rationalistic and evolutionist philosophy of history. Although this optimism seems unrealistic today, modern western culture has to maintain it, at any rate ideologically and rhetorically.

Confronted with the Christian tradition, modern liberal ideology must disregard the Christian eschatology, define Christian dogma as a sort of illusionary religious notion, and reject the Christian kerygma with its claim to represent the absolute and permanent truth. Until recent decades the Scandinavian democracies retained the Christian religion as an integral part of their ideological foundation, but today this situation is dramatically changed. The Christian tradition is no longer the absolute official ideology of the State, determining the legislation and administration of society, but the State still finds it culturally and politically opportune to allow new generations to be acquainted with the Christian tradition, its texts and its values. From a certain perspective the Scandinavian States are in some ways Protestant cultural States, but at the same time it cannot be denied that they have mostly abandoned their Christian heritage. The law of free abortion and the legal acceptance and registration of homosexual relationships as a counterpart to the traditional marriage are examples illustrating a process of deep secularisation.

IV

The Lutheran tradition still survives in modern democratic society, but at the same time it must be realised that some of the most important theological ideas of the Lutheran tradition are now losing their determining role even in the Lutheran Church itself. The impressive fact is that these very ideas were the ones which caused the most serious controversy with the Roman Catholics during the sixteenth century. At the same time a change in the ecumenical situation has taken place, and its consequences have to be thoroughly considered.

What brought Luther in conflict first of all with the highest administration of the Church was his stubborn and uncompromising assertion that Holy Scripture should be the exclusive authority for the Church in questions concerning Christian faith and life. It cannot be ignored that the understanding of scriptural authority in the Reformation is in many ways very different from the modern Lutheran one. For Luther, Scripture is sufficient as the only source and norm for faith and doctrines: Scripture can function in this way because its textual meaning is lucid and plain. So it was for the Fathers of the Reformation and later on for the Lutheran orthodoxy of the seventeenth century.[12] In Lutheran theology today the original concept of *claritas Scripturae* is mostly absent, or it is misinterpreted in accordance with a modern hermeneutic, which finds the '*claritas*' in the correlation between the scriptural message and the individual's religious experience, a view far removed from the concept of scriptural authority in the Reformation.

For Luther the doctrine of *claritas Scripturae* was defined in two ways. Firstly, it is possible to perceive the objective meaning of the scriptural content in the text alone. The theologians of the Lutheran Reformation not only maintained the conventional rule that the obscurities in Scripture should be elucidated by the clear texts, but they also asserted that the metaphorical and allegorical interpretation must be regarded as secondary when dogmatic or confessional issues have to be decided. Luther himself was very sceptical about this kind of biblical interpretation. It is by means of a linguistic analysis of the biblical text, in order to elucidate its plain meaning, that the Church develops her doctrine and message. Secondly, the

Lutheran concept of *claritas Scripturae* presupposes that Scripture has a dynamic function in the Church and the world. Scripture is a 'light', which creates clarity in our minds and elucidates our life, cf. Pss. 19. 8; 119. 105. As the Psalmist says: 'Your word is a lamp to my feet and a light for my path'.[13] This dynamic understanding of Scripture issues in the typical Lutheran doctrine of Scripture as a self-interpreting subject. In Luther's understanding of Scripture we can observe influences from the late Middle Ages and humanism, but primarily he transmits ideas about communication from the early Middle Ages. At that time, and as a consequence of the socio-political nature of that society, the secret and hidden represents disintegrating demonic powers. On the other hand the manifest and the public, which can be perceived and observed by all, is consequently of high moral standard and value. This understanding of society and of political communication corresponds with the biblical dualism of light and darkness, truth and falsehood, which is particularly evident in the Gospel of John and which is apocalyptically unfolded in the Augustinian theology of history. In the theology of Luther we encounter this positive evaluation of what is public and manifest and known to all, and his concept of *claritas Scripturae* is an aspect of this.[14]

In the modern Lutheran state Churches the Lutheran theologians usually assert the exclusive authority of Scripture, but the conditions for a genuine transmission of the original reformation understanding of Scripture are not present, either in the cultural context or in the state Church herself. The modern established Church, united with the liberal democracy, cannot accept the theological dualism of revealed truth and demonic falsehood, light and darkness, because the dualism in modern society is principally between rationality and the irrational things, reaction and progress. In such a cultural context it is therefore impossible to perceive that a text in itself has an objective and plain meaning and has to be accepted as such. On the contrary, the text must, and necessarily will be, interpreted first of all by the individual and later on within a community of discourse. Ultimately the meaning of the text is constituted by the process of interpretation, because no objective textual meaning can be found. The ideological effect of this relativism is the lack of rationality in modern democratic society. The theological effect is that the truth of Scripture depends on the correlation between the scriptural message and the spirituality of the human community. To formulate it in another way, it depends on the integration or synthesis of the spiritual meaning of the biblical texts and the moral and religious spirit of the contemporary culture. This kind of hermeneutic is in conflict not only with the original Lutheran doctrine of Scripture, but with Lutheran anthropology as well.

Because the Lutheran Church and her theology are determined in reality by the ecclesial structure of the modern state Church, the Lutheran tradition is afflicted by an acute process of democratisation, which in the long run leads to a misinterpretation of dogma and to the suspension of biblical morality as obsolete, since the authority of the Scripture has faded away. One of the most deeply felt problems in the Lutheran world today is therefore inevitably the quest for Authority. But how can Authority be found, when its ideological basis has disintegrated, and its institutional framework is weak and unreliable because of the state Churches? These Churches are at the disposal of the secular majority in society and the rulers of the modern State. These are in return eager to use their power over the Church, and the leaders of the state Churches – either installed by or acceptable to the secular state authorities – co-operate more or less enthusiastically with the secular powers.

How could the Lutheran Churches so easily both accept the secularisation of the State and co-operate with it, when the consequences of such a process are so fateful ? To find a clear explanation is difficult, as the question is very complex, and has implicitly both ideological and political aspects. But some central characteristics of Reformation theology cannot be neglected. One of the slogans of the Reformation was *sola scriptura*; another one was *sola fide*. This latter expresses the Lutheran doctrine of justification by faith alone. We must concentrate on this doctrinal core of the Reformation, if we are to find the causes of the theological and spiritual breakdown of the Lutheran tradition.

We are justified by faith alone. This sentence is the central message of Lutheran theology. The justification of the believer is understood as a forensic act of God, giving humans the righteousness of Christ.[15] Although Lutheran theologians have always discussed the relationship between the forensic and the effective aspects of justification, it is obvious that the forensic understanding represents the fundamental perspective in the Lutheran theology. All other theological topics, especially in ethics and ecclesiology, are understood from this point of view, and questions concerning the structure of the Church, for example the relationship between Church and State, must be solved in harmony with the doctrine of justification. One consequence is the Lutheran concept of *adiaphora*. The relationship to the State, seen from the perspective of *adiaphora*, is principally a non-doctrinal question, because the structures of the Church are theologically indifferent, if the administration of the Word of God and the sacraments are to be free. The implication of the pragmatic Lutheran view about *adiaphora* is that the Church must be essentially understood as an institution in the service of a religious administration, and consequently she tends to be neglected as *communio*. In a social-democratic society the consequences of such an ecclesiology are obvious. From a social-democratic point of view an established Church must be regarded as a part of the welfare State, paid to meet the religious needs of the people. Under these conditions such a Church is acceptable if her message is not too provocative, and if consequently the *communio* is not allowed in principle to separate itself from the civil society, but instead is fully integrated. The State intends to control and administer social life, and therefore no social sector may remain protected from official influence. A Church, which tries to uphold among her members certain religious and moral standards which differ from the secular ones, will in a social democratic society meet grave difficulties, because the integration of the population into one social body is so intensive. If the state authorities in addition have the right to govern the Church, the spiritual integrity of the Christian community within the Church will be almost impossible to maintain. In their social and political life the members of the Church will be confronted with the secularising State, and in the Church they will meet the same State administering the Church in order to harmonise Christian and secular standards of faith and morals.

The doctrine of justification by faith alone produced during the era of the Reformation the freedom to stand up against suppression by ecclesiastical and secular authorities. In modern Lutheran theology the same doctrine enables divergence from genuine ecclesial tradition and authority, and at the same time it enables institutional and ideological accommodation to secularisation. Based on the Lutheran doctrine of justification modern theology criticises and tries to emancipate the Church from the traditional structure of ministry, dogma and morals. The critique inevitably attacks the ecclesial tradition, and the written Word of God as well, since apostolic authority is not as such accepted. In Scripture critics find a variety of, and as they see it, conflicting theological concepts. In addition they conclude that Scripture primarily reflects the social and ideological conditions of ancient times. For modern theology scriptural authority is in the end an insoluble problem. The radical wing of Lutheran theology tries to find a way out of it by understanding 'apostolic' as a Christian message which, once emancipated from ancient doctrine, structures and morals, can be opened up for a new future, whose content is unknown, but essentially positive. In this way the doctrine of justification turns out to be a modern 'therapeutic' message of freedom in line with the ideas of the Enlightenment in general. And Lutheran theology runs the risk of being a vague utopian ideology incompatible with biblical faith and doctrine. In many Lutheran Churches we can already observe such apostasy. From a contextual point of view the Lutheran Churches are caught in a trap, because of their one-sided interpretation of their own Reformation tradition.

V

Are we then seeing the end of the Protestant story ? Many hold a contrary view and proclaim Protestantism as a Christianity for the future. A political or cultural success provides no standard of judging the truth of a doctrinal position: the important thing is to be faithful to the apostolic message and doctrine. The criteria of theological truth are its apostolicity and catholicity. The Lutheran Reformation intended to be faithful to the apostolic foundation of the universal Church and her genuine catholic tradition. But because of the ecumenical collapse during the century of the Reformation the ecumenical aspect of the Lutheran position faded away, and all the participants in the spiritual conflicts of the time developed into confessional Churches, with even the old Roman Catholic Church having to identify herself in a confessional sense. Since the Lutheran Reformation had to place itself under the protection of the secular powers, the ecumenical approach was blocked, and the confessional Lutheran Churches were all national and territorial, united with and governed by the secular national state. The effect was in the long run fatal, not only institutionally and politically, but theologically and doctrinally too. If we look at the theological developments within the Lutheran tradition from a critical perspective, we can regard the mainstream of Lutheran theology as an attempt to justify the synthesis between the Church and State and as a solution to the problems caused by this political arrangement.

The Lutheran theology of our own day must take up its task where the Reformation collapsed, starting the renewal of apostolic and catholic faith and doctrine within a Lutheran framework. This cannot be done on the basis of the paradigm of the modern Lutheran theology. On the contrary we have to recapture the witness of the Diet of Augsburg in 1530: 'This is about the sum of our teaching, in which it can be seen that there is nothing which departs from the Scriptures or the universal Church or the Church of Rome....'[16] and from that position walk forward together with Christians who share the same commitment.

Notes

1. Berndt Hamm / Bernd Moeller / Dorothea Wendebourg, *Reformationstheorien* (Göttingen, 1995).
2. Wolfgang Höhne, *Luthers Anschauung über die Kontinuität der Kirche* (Berlin-Hamburg, 1963).
3. Peter Fraenkel, 'Revelation and Tradition. Notes on Some Aspects of Doctrinal Continuity in the Theology of Philip Melanchthon', *Studia Theologica* (1959), pp.97–133.

4. Confessio Augustana, article XXVIII, *The Book of Concorde* (Philadelphia, 1959), pp.81–96; Bernt T. Oftestad, 'Bishop, Congregation, and Authority in Article 28 of the Augsburg Confession', *Lutheran Quarterly*, VIII/2 (1994), pp.163–180.
5. Thomas A. Brady, Jr., Heiko Oberman, James D. Tracy, eds., *Handbook of European History 1400–1600. Late Middle Ages, Renaissance and Reformation I* (Leiden-New York-Cologne, 1994), pp.XIII–XXIV.
6. Martin Heckel, 'Die reichsrechtliche Bedeutung der Bekenntnisse', in M. Brecht / R. Schwartz, *Bekenntnis und Einheit der Kirche* (Stuttgart, 1980), pp.57–88.
7. Martin Brecht, ed., *Martin Luther und das Bischofsamt* (Stuttgart, 1990).
8. Martin Schwartz Lausten, *Reformationen i Danmark* (Copenhagen, 1987); Bernt T. Oftestad, Tarald Rasmussen and Jan Schumacher, *Norsk kirkehistorie* (Oslo, 1991), pp.83–112.
9. ibid.
10. ibid. pp.177–297.
11. Jürgen Habermas, *Strukturwandel der Öffentlichkeit* (Darmstad, 1980).
12. *The Book of Concorde*, op. cit., pp.464ff.
13. Friedrich Beisser, *Claritas Scripturae bei Martin Luther* (Göttingen, 1966).
14. Andreas Gestrich, *Absolutismus und Öffentlichkeit* (Göttingen, 1994), pp.34–68; Bernt T. Oftestad, 'Öffentliches Amt und kirchliche Gemeinschaft – Luthers theologische Auslegung des Begriffs "öffentlich" ' in Bengt Hägglund and Gerhard Müller, *Kirche in der Schule Luthers* (Erlangen, 1995), pp.90–102.
15. Confessio Augustana, article IV, *The Book of Concorde*, op. cit., p.30.
16. '*Haec fere summa est doctrinae apud nos, in qua cerni potest nihil inesse, quod discrepet a scripturis vel ab ecclesia catholica vel ab ecclesia Romana.*' *The Book of Concorde*, op. cit., p.47.

The Soul is Dead that Slumbers (Longfellow)

George Austin

In 1987 an extraordinary book became the No.1 best-seller in the United States. It was 'The Closing of the American Mind' by a distinguished professor, Allan Bloom, in which he showed clearly how higher education had in the previous two decades failed democracy and impoverished the souls of a generation of students.

At the heart of the problem which he identified among those in higher education was the almost universally accepted concept that truth is relative. This was regarded 'not as a theoretical insight but a moral postulate, the condition of a free society, or so they see it.' Absolutism was seen as the only possible alternative to relativism, and what they feared from it was not error but intolerance. The true believer, in other words, was the real danger. The purpose of their education was 'not to make them scholars but to provide them with a moral virtue – openness.' 'There is no enemy other than the man who is not open to everything.'

But it was not openness as we once understood it, for 'openness used to be the virtue that permitted us to seek the good by using reason.' Now it meant 'accepting everything and denying reason's power.' In other words, Bloom said, 'Openness to closedness is what we teach.'

Bloom's thesis related to the situation in the American universities. But no one closely involved in the life of the Churches, either in the United States or in Britain, could fail to detect accurate parallels in the problems which Christians also face within the religious institutions which they serve, not least the Church of England.

'What is truth?' asked Pontius Pilate of Jesus. The Anglican Church has always had a reputation as a tolerant body. It does not go in for heresy hunts and even allows its bishops, the supposed guardians of the faith, sometimes to stray well beyond the boundaries which it has set up.

For whatever might sometimes be claimed, there are boundaries, set out in its affirmation of the creeds of the Church, Holy Scripture, and the doctrine contained in the Book of Common Prayer and the Ordinal, and even though a breadth of interpretation is allowed (for who can fully comprehend the mysteries of a God who is the creator of all that is?), there is an absolutism which requires that such interpretation be kept with the boundaries set out by those four foundation documents. It is not a free for all – or at least it is not supposed to be.

Even so, the former Bishop of Durham received no official rebuke, only prolonged applause, when in a speech in a General Synod debate in July 1986 on the 'Nature of Christian Belief' (a speech he later repeated in a book) he dismissed the traditional concept of a physical resurrection as being 'in danger of implying, or actually portraying, a God who is, at the best, a cultic idol, and at the worst, the very devil.'

Indeed in the present climate in the Church of England it is much more likely that a traditional believer, one who accepts and proclaims that which has always been taught by the Church down the ages, will be dismissed or ridiculed as an unthinking fundamentalist than a bishop whose questioning may stray beyond doctrinal boundaries will be rebuked for what in official Anglican terms is undoubtedly false teaching.

It is not that heresy is a dirty word, to be avoided by those whose philosophy demands openness to all views. Archbishop George Carey was quick to denounce with that very same word those who could not accept the new dogma that a woman can be ordained priest, a teaching certainly not held by all Christians at all times. It appeared to matter little to him that he was in effect excommunicating from orthodox belief not only two-thirds of Christians of the present day, but also the entire Catholic and Orthodox constituency who had lived and worshipped in the two thousand years since the birth of Christ.

Just as the truth of fundamental doctrine is now regarded as relative, so too is the commitment to the ethical behaviour and standards required by scriptural precepts. God no longer writes the Church's agenda; it is written by the world which he created and found it necessary to come into to redeem. Biblical standards are but one benchmark against which to measure behaviour, and a flawed benchmark at that, since cultural relativism demands that nothing from one age can be binding upon the next.

But relativism is little more than a symptom of the disease within the Church, though it has aggravated the sickness. As the much-trumpeted Decade of Evangelism limps to its close, the Church of England continues to lose money, members and ministers at an alarming and accelerating rate. Bishops will sometimes dismiss suggestions of decline in terms which bring to mind the comments of King Edward VII to the Prime Minister of the day about a south coast Rector. 'You really ought to make that man a bishop. Whenever I go to his Church, it's always packed to the doors.'

Yet the decline is certainly irregular. Statistics only produce averages, and the declining Churches can hide the reality of growth. For growth there is, especially in charismatic (and non-charismatic) evangelical Churches, and if the outward expression of phenomena like the Toronto blessing is not to everyone's taste – and has its questionable side – one cannot deny that the Holy Spirit has blessed such Churches.

There is the evangelical charismatic Church of St Michael-le-Belfry in York, and one can only thank God for what is happening there, aided not a little by the acceptance among its people that not everyone comes to God in the same way. Financially it attracts the highest quota in the diocese; but the second highest is the very different parish of Cottingham. Moderately Catholic in its worship, it attracts a large congregation, including students from the nearby Hull University. An average of seventeen people came to daily Mass throughout 1995, and in Lent nearly thirty a day. There cannot be many Churches in England which could make such a claim.

In the city of York there is too the parish of St Luke's, by no means rich and not far from an urban priority classification. Evangelical/Catholic in its tradition (incense and guitars in popular-speak), it is full every Sunday, with a congregation from every age-group.

Outside the diocese of York there is the parish of St Peter's Bushey Heath, which, since the departure of its ancient and out-dated vicar (the author of this essay), has doubled its electoral roll membership, tripled its Easter attendances, and more than quadrupled its Christmas congregations under the leadership of its vicar, Robbie Low. As in all four parishes, a firm, orthodox, biblical faith is taught by Fr. Low, and he has been told in no uncertain terms that, for his pains, he has ruled himself out for future preferment. 'You will never get another job in this diocese.' So much for the Decade of Evangelism.

In all these parishes, it is the teaching of orthodox faith which is the common factor, not that in one the worship is traditional, and in others charismatic with guitars and Mission Praise, nor the presence or absence of catholic ceremonial. It is the faith which attracts and inspires, and brings worshippers of every age-group and background.

But that should not be a surprise, if the Gospel is truly the Good News that it is. The surprise is that people actually attend and sometimes give vocal support where their priest teaches a liberal mish-mash which casts doubts upon the Incarnation and Resurrection and other primary articles of faith, or where he diminishes the reality of sin and consequently cannot offer redemption for something which is absent in the first place.

Friendship and familiarity are of course powerful attractions, and for a time can mask a shallowness of faith. But only for a time. In the end, there really is no reason to attend a Church which has lost the only *raison d'être* which gives it meaning and force. Yet the theological and moral relativism which for at least three decades has afflicted the Church of England (and the Church of England is not alone in this) has infected and inspired a whole generation of clergy.

Bishop Michael Baughan of Chester has more than once complained that in the non-residential courses, claiming as they do to cross theological party boundaries, it is too often the catholic who will teach liturgy and pastoralia, and the evangelical who will teach Church history, but the liberal who will deal with doctrine and ethics.

A deacon who had trained under one such course told how she had been to two sessions on the sacrament of holy matrimony, of which one was entirely given over to the production of a liturgy for same-sex marriages. A confidential report on an ordinand from a theological college, sent to the bishop who was to ordain him, complained that the young man had vigorously and obstinately resisted all attempts to lead him away from out-dated theological concepts and towards the acceptance of the new insights of the modern 'understanding'. He was clearly a man of integrity and courage, and we cannot know how many others, who for greater safety and a quiet life, simply write their examination papers with the heresies acceptable to their teachers without taking them on board in their own lives and beliefs.

Although in the promise that against the Church of God even the gates of hell would not prevail, nothing was said about the Anglican Church, there are signs of hope for the future and it is right that we should give that the emphasis in this essay, and with the fact that it is from the proclamation of a biblical faith that growth will and does come.

It is significant too that leadership in the determinedly orthodox groups like Forward in Faith and Cost of Conscience on the catholic wing and Reform on the evangelical is firmly in the hands of parochial clergy and not with the bishops, who – if they are there at all – are peripheral to the movements themselves. There is in fact something distinctly odd about the nature of Episcopal leadership.

It is not that relativism runs riot among the bench of bishops. Indeed, it is fair to say that in recent years there has been a distinct shift from the days of Runcie's primacy when, in Canon Gareth Bennett's famous description, there was in the Archbishop a

'clear preference for men of liberal disposition with a moderately Catholic style which is not taken to the point of having firm principles. If in addition they have a good appearance and are articulate over the media he is prepared to overlook a certain theological deficiency. Dr. Runcie and his closest associates are men who have nothing to prevent them following what they think is the wish of the majority of the moment.'

It was a devastatingly accurate description of the leadership of

the Church of England in the mid-1980s and it was a development which was the foundation of the present crisis in which
the Church finds itself. It was not confined to the bench of
bishops, diocesan or suffragan, but spread downwards to the
middle management of advisers, a group whose numbers had
grown like a cancer in the Runcie period, and whose influence
still pervades the Church.

Yet there has certainly been a distinct shift, at any rate at the
episcopal level. Runcie no doubt believed – and with some justification, for they were able men at any rate within the limitations
of his prejudices – that he had appointed the next generation of
senior Church leaders. Significantly not one of them has moved
to any of the greater sees of Canterbury, York, London,
Winchester and Durham, nor to larger dioceses like
Chelmsford. Astonishingly, half of these vacancies were filled
directly from among the suffragans, which says something about
the legacy left behind by the disastrous policies of the 1980s.

Unfortunately the concept of collegiality is proving a more
difficult obstacle for the bishops to overcome, even if they had
the will so to do. Archbishop Runcie probably saw collegiality as a means whereby the bishops would speak with one
voice and thereby restore an episcopal lead (and role) to a
synodical Church. It has not worked like that, but has instead
become a ball and chain which has crippled the bishops almost
entirely from exercising leadership of any real significance. 'I
can't get a single bishop to make a comment' is a common
despairing cry from journalists when moral and theological
issues hit the headlines.

No doubt if they did they would be taken to task by their
peers when next they met for daring to break ranks – as one
incautious archdeacon from the Province of Canterbury was
rebuked recently for speaking out of turn. He had appeared on
television to make a biblical stand on a moral issue and was
told in no uncertain terms that if he hoped for future preferment he must not do so again.

It is little wonder then that when bishops do attempt to take
the lead, even with orthodox clergy groupings, they are so
often rebuffed. Too much water has passed under the wrong
bridges for many of them ever to be fully trusted.

Even though the Church of England is an episcopal Church,

this need not matter, and could be the Church's gain. Bishops run dioceses, and while they still live in vast palaces they will always seem a little remote from their people; deans run cathedrals, which at their best illustrate the heights to which Christian worship can aspire; archdeacons keep the wheels of the Church well-oiled and are at their most useful when they are the least visible. But the real work of the Church, which is the pastoral care of God's people, Churchgoing and non-Churchgoing, is in the parishes, with the clergy preaching, teaching, guiding, enabling the people of God to exercise the whole ministry of the Church.

Forward in Faith clergy and those who belong to Reform sometimes bewail the fact that none of their number is ever again likely to be appointed to senior office within the Church. And they are right. It would be almost impossible for a parish priest who supported the aims of either body to squeeze through that Crown Appointments Commission net which protects the diocesan bench from undesirable elements. It is clear too that solemn promises given at the time of the passing of the ordination of women measure that every diocese would be encouraged to appoint someone from the orthodox integrity to its suffragan staff has been conspicuously, continuously and deliberately broken.

But what Forward in Faith and Reform must take into their hearts and minds is that it does not matter. The Church of England will be renewed (if it is God's will that it should be renewed) from, by, and in the parishes, by the proclaiming of an orthodox gospel and a biblical morality, and in no other way. And if the Church sinks into heresy and apostasy as the Episcopal Church of America has done on so many issues, the Church of England, in contrast, does have its Trojan horse in the Provincial Episcopal Visitors, the 'flying bishops', who can and must proclaim, with as loud a voice as possible when the Church moves into error, 'This does not happen in our part of the Church, in the parishes which we serve. If you don't like it, come and join us.'

The threat of theological and moral relativism is still there, stronger than ever, and there is the example of England's sister Church across the Atlantic to give warning, by its clear example, of all the dangers.

Already the pleas for a recognition of gay lifestyles as compatible with Christian belief are well over the horizon, supported by such a formidable figure in Anglicanism as Archbishop Desmond Tutu, and part of the agenda of Affirming Catholicism, whose chairman is the Bishop of Salisbury.

Already the General Synod has required the Liturgical Commission to remove masculine pronouns for God from new services, preparing the ground for the final battle to de-Christianise God.

Already when orthodox priests move from parishes, they are all too often deliberately replaced by less orthodox successors, so that the many younger Forward in Faith clergy are asking if there really is any place for them in the future in the Church of England. Already promises made and assurances given that liberal bishops would appoint suffragans of both integrities, and that deaneries would have at least one parish where the priest was of the second integrity, have been largely abandoned.

Already laity are feeling marginalised in some parishes if they speak out for traditional values and beliefs, marginalised by clergy who despise their 'obstinacy'.

There is far to go before England matches the overt and persistent persecution which orthodox clergy and laity suffer in Canada and the United States. But the danger signals are there and the example clear for both sides to see and take note of for future reference. If it comes to the Church of England, it will be the final skirmish for the soul of the Church, when its orthodox members, clergy and laity, will fight not against flesh and blood but against the powers and principalities of the darkness of this world.

The Church of England may lose, as it appears orthodoxy in the Episcopal Church of the USA is in its final death throes. But there must be no despair and the fight for truth over falsehood must not be abandoned. It was for this very time that the call to serve, to follow Christ, came in the first place. It is part of the cross which must be borne, for though the Church of England may be destroyed by these dark forces, the Church of God cannot be destroyed. The final battle has already been fought, and that battle was won decisively by Jesus Christ on the cross of Calvary.

Broken Promises – the Nordic Decline

Dag Sandahl

Recently a friend showed me a Swedish religious textbook written for high-school level pupils, aged 18–19. Not for the first time I realised how important it is to understand what sort of knowledge and values are being imparted to young people and how easy it is to understand contemporary 'political correctness' by looking at the school curriculum and reading the books the students have to read. It is not only the mathematics teachers in Nazi Germany, calculating the costs of dealing with people with mental illnesses, who provide valuable political insights!

In this book very little is said about Christian doctrine, as ethical questions dominate. But there are some obviously important doctrinal statements, such as 'the Old Testament was written by men, for men'.

What this is supposed to mean exactly is perhaps not very clear, but the impression is that a book such as the Old Testament must be irrelevant, and that the Old Testament certainly cannot be regarded as divinely inspired. It is ancient literature, written *by* men, *for* men. When I am in a bad mood I remember the slogan in Nazi Germany: '*by* Jews, *for* Jews'. The message in both cases is clear. The Old Testament is irrelevant, and a clever high-school student will understand that the same argument can be used against the New Testament. It is written *by* men, *for* men. So why bother with the Bible?

They will however be given certain facts about the current situation, that in Sweden there is still strong opposition against women priests. There are male priests who refuse to wear any vestments which have been used by a woman priest, and who will use incense to cleanse a church after a woman priest has conducted a service in it. However when the controversy about the ordination of women is referred to in education it will not be analysed in any way, or even explained. There will just be references to rumours. But if the student asks about how opponents to women's ordination behave, there will be just one official answer: they act like oppressors.

There is another aspect of the situation which yields important insights. In Sweden the ordination of women is a basic doctrine of the 'Modern Project' and the religious system based on it. This was already evident in 1938, when the most important Swedish organisations for women's rights, in different political parties and trades unions, passed a resolution to the Government. The debate about ministry within the Church never touched on the underlying political questions or on the issue of what type of religion the Modern Project would create.

Old slogans – today's values

With the beginning of the Enlightenment and the French Revolution a popular religious system had arrived at its dogma: God, morality, immortality as a reward of virtue, and the exclusion of religious intolerance (J-J Rousseau, *The Social Contract*, Book 4, Chapter 8). Religious intolerance in Europe since then has been identified, by definition, with the Church and her values, and measures have been taken in most European countries against the Church, in various forms, ideologically and/or legally. An institution which had been regarded as a dominant source of ideology for the State has been succeeded by others, primarily the public school where basic values are taught.

The Modern Project, the agenda for the Swedish welfare State, is rooted in the Enlightenment and is based on its values, and it is the means of delivering contemporary ideology and values to the people. In this the school system plays an important role. Although a country may be superficially multicultural, there will essentially be *one* popular culture which will create common values. The Church may be used by this system to some extent as a co-operator in building the modern society, but her confessions or traditions will not be allowed to affect the Modern Project. So as an issue of political truth, the high school students will not be given correct information about the Old Testament or about how those opposed to women priests actually behave.

However, another pattern from the time of the French Revolution also emerges. Then the people knew who was a good priest (*bon prêtre*), and when they really needed to they used him to baptise their child and to bury Grandma. The implication is clear: the people, or at least some of them, knew where to find the spiritual guidance they needed after the religious system and basic values were changed. There will always be people like that. The problem is not the people, but a ruling class, and the values and information that this class, who dominate the media and control the process of selecting bishops and administrators in the Church, transmit to the people.

A Church unable to understand the contemporary situation: Church and Politics

When debating the issue of ordination in the Swedish Parliament in 1958, a liberal MP frankly declared himself to be 'by no means a Lutheran' but saw the MPs nevertheless as the Church people. 'We are the representatives of the Church of Sweden as much as the General Synod or the so-called faithful in the Church. We have to make decisions in this matter, sooner or later, because we are the Church.' One newspaper's editorial regarded the decisions taken by the Government and the Parliament as parallel to the Lutheran Reformation, preventing a reactionary conversion of the Church to Roman Catholicism. When the first woman bishop in Norway was appointed by the Government a spokesman said 'The State takes the lead. The Church follows.' The same political pattern can be seen in both countries.

To define a controversy about ministry in that situation as a theological dispute is basically to misunderstand what is happening. Theology presupposes a faith which wants to understand God's will. In the Nordic countries political decisions are based on contemporary ideology, not theology. That is how they are arrived at, and that is why political weapons are used to deal with minorities.

Learning from the Reformation – Church and Power

Evangelical Lutheran Churches commemorate Martin Luther but seldom recognise that the Reformation was not simply a question about theology but about structures, institutions and power, and about a deep concern for people's spiritual needs. Martin Luther never intended to start a reformation. He started a process which led from academic discussions to the people. The issues about indulgences were explosive because they had severe economic consequences for Rome. The structure could not handle what happened but was forced to ban Luther. Structures, institutions and power act like that. A Church named after Martin Luther ought to be sensitive to every tendency to act like an institution by defending its own interests. And when politics are openly involved in making decisions about faith and order, this is the classic stimulus to reformation and renewal. The historical experience of 1517 and after offers tools for a Church which is willing to ask for God's call and for the insight to understand the spiritual needs of the people.

When fellow Christians become 'counterparts'

The current situation in the Church of Sweden is that no one will be ordained to the priesthood unless he is willing to co-operate liturgically with a woman priest. The bishop of Växjö said that the precondition for ordination is that candidates must be prepared to distribute the chalice when a woman priest is celebrating. He also broke his predecessor's written promises to ordain candidates, who have received a complete theological education, but are refused access to the final pastoral seminary. The tacit implication for all dissident priests is 'We don't want you. If you had been a student now the bishop would refuse to ordain you.' That is a message which undermines an overworked priest.

In the diocese of Lund there was a deacon who worked temporarily as a parish assistant. He attended two masses celebrated by the woman vicar without taking communion. She asked why and suddenly realised that he was an opponent of women's ordination. The deacon declared himself willing to co-operate in whatever ways he was able, but was sacked a week later, having been accused of not declaring his position. That nobody had asked what it was, was irrelevant. If he *had* been asked, the deacon would of course have been given no opportunity to work in that parish.

In my deanery a woman (aged about forty and a mother of four) was elected to the PCC, and at the first PCC meeting she was elected chairman. One year later she was asked her opinion about women priests; she declared herself to be an opponent. When asked to resign she refused. In this situation four members of the PCC decided to resign, and that of course made headlines in the local papers.

What is demonstrated by these examples is a strategy whereby opponents are rendered invisible. The method of achieving that outcome is a familiar one. It involves not only lies and actions which marginalise and eliminate the enemy, but also a silent and perhaps uncomfortable majority who lack the courage to protest but who stay silent, hoping for better times (often invoking the name of God in order to avoid taking a stand, with the risks that this would imply).

For years we have had well orchestrated political elections of bishops – and Government approval has ensured that only those in favour of women's ordination have become bishops. This policy has meant that ordinary priests will now be asked for their opinion about women priests when, for instance, they apply for a parish. This does not only apply to priests, as has become apparent. To date the most extreme example has been that of a parish engaging a cleaner: the first question put to the applicants was about the ordination of women. If you are a dissident you are not suitable to do the cleaning.

The bishops can regret the present situation but never understand in what way *they* created it or prepared for it by remaining silent. The experience of the minority is always the same: discussions and serious attempts to reach solutions always create more problems. The latest example, from 1993, is of a committee (including representatives from the Bishops' Conference, the Central Board, Church Union and the Free Synod) which produced a report called *Church – Ministry – Unity*. When it was published the bishops demanded that no one should declare ordinations of women invalid, and the General Synod tightened up that demand by insisting that everyone should actively acknowledge such ordinations. The promises given in 1958 and the so-called conscience clause are now null and utterly void!

It is not clear to what extent the bishops believe that a firm position on their part will change the mind of the opposition. I am afraid that what is really happening is that we are losing the opportunity to make Christ known in this country. And we have lost a great deal of ground so far: fellow Christians have become counterparts to each other, divided into 'us' and 'them'. A man working on a diocesan staff recently made a statement on a TV debate about homosexuality which illustrates this: he said 'People who regard the Bible as the Word of God must be full of hate'.

The insight that the inclusive Church can offer a home to everybody except those who believe in God and go to Church every Sunday is not surprising. The Church often has greater difficulties with people of faith than with people with little, or no, faith. When under political pressure it is quite logical to discuss who can stay in the Church and who ought to leave. That is not an uncommon discussion now – although for a priest trained in the 60's or 70's, and encountering the debate at that time about being an inclusive Church, it is in many ways a strange experience.

A Church changed to a sect

Bishop Anders Nygren has declared that the Church of Sweden has switched to an alien – a gnostic – track. Obviously the Church is acting in a sectarian way in relation to a minority. The members who do not fit in with the patterns manifested by the majority will be asked to leave. And there is nothing to obstruct their portrayal as evil Christians – describing them in a way that would not be true even given that human weakness is the condition under which they live. It is a classic way of ruling.

A Church can be transformed into a sect: a majority sect. In Norway some very outspoken debates over priests in conflict with a political majority have led to free parishes being set up within the Church of Norway, without a formal break and the creation of a denomination. The Norwegians have lived for a long time with a tradition of resistance against the political power exercised from Denmark or the Central Bureaucracy in Oslo. The fisherman, the farmer and the teacher have never been used to obeying instructions from Copenhagen or Oslo: they followed good old traditions and turned their backs on modernism. Friedrich Engels paid homage to this attitude, and without reference to this historical tradition it will never be understood how priests can establish new free parishes within the Church system and without asking for permission to do so.

Swedish society is different. From the sixteenth century it developed a strong central Government with governors ensuring the intentions of the central power were implemented. Local movements opposing that policy were defeated by hired knights and repression in areas in opposition was severe. The State controls the people in a well organised country. Out of that historical experience it will take some time before people say 'Now, it is enough.'

With the reference to Friedrich Engels we return to an underlying theme: opposing the ruling class and being faithful to the classic Christian faith is to stand with the people. This was true at the time of the French Revolution and it is still true now. And some people will look at that deep solidarity with the Gospel and with the people, and will understand the connection. When the leaders of the uprising against the king were executed in 1543 there were some priests among them.

What is new about the situation in both Sweden and Norway is that the question of ordaining women to the episcopacy and priesthood has been a watershed, but even more it has been a revelation. We have a situation which cannot last for long. A Church in a secularised culture such as the Swedish or the Norwegian one cannot reach the people by amputating her catholic wing. The reason is very simple and not primarily theological: a system which expels unacceptable people will attract no one. The secondary reason, though, is of course theological. The Church must be a catholic Church. It is intrinsic to her very nature.

In Sweden and Norway we are now being forced to ask basic questions not only about what faith really means but also to 'discern the spirits'. We need to ask about the methods being used in the Churches to keep a minority down. When the leaders of the Church use a combination of lies, casting of suspicion, broken promises and pure violence in bureaucratic form in order to secure a reform – whose Spirit stands behind this? And whose Spirit forces bishops and other church leaders to remain silent when lies about their fellow Christians are voiced? Faith will always be tested in relation to people and practice, and some of us will be forced to draw the conclusion that God never acts like this. These politics are not true to the identity of the Church. Understanding that is to stand together with Martin Luther.

A witness for the Truth

The challenge for the Nordic Churches is to revive something which once gave the Churches a natural position in the people's life. It is mostly, I think, a matter of self-confidence, the result of her understanding of her own identity and vocation.

Faithful to the heritage

In Sweden and Norway the faithful people attending church on Sundays form a small religious minority within a nominally strong Church. In some parishes 0.7% of the population come to the services. The average figure in Sweden is 2%. From this it will be apparent that in the future there will be a lack of people attending services, but also, within a few years, a decline in membership of local PCCs. So far the political parties have supplied the PCCs with people but now there are not enough people (as I have said elsewhere, the parties no longer have so many retired members...) and people born in the 20's and later cannot be expected to suddenly start partic- ipating in parish life. From this perspective it is valuable to have had the experience of being a member of a minority, with experience of the sort of thing which happens in that situation.

To behave like the majority in conforming to cultural patterns – which it is easy to understand is a temptation for a declining Church – is to fool oneself. Whatever doctrinal posi- tion a Church takes, it will remain a minority in secularised western Europe. What are needed now are new insights about the serious situation in which the Church lives: pastoral failure, alarming statistical, and to some extent economic, data, national Churches on the verge of collapse, and an incredible inability to deal with issues which threaten the unity of the Church.

There are analyses and suggestions, experiences and insights which could be useful. However decisions already taken mean that all these possibilities have to be subordinated to one single fundamental question, the fundamental question for a religion which is part of the Modern Project and which has been turned into an ideology. The question is to what extent classical Christian beliefs can survive at all. Perhaps we already have seen a shift of religion within the system. The symbols and the doctrines not under debate remain, but the contents are differ- ent: God, morality, immortality as a reward of virtue and the exclusion of religious intolerance. The parish priest very often does not see this, and not having alternatives he protects himself by not understanding the situation, but spending his time nurturing and caring for his parish. In this situation such a limited agenda does not work. Martin Luther understood that his responsibility was not limited to Wittenberg but extended to the Catholic Church as a whole.

Faithful to the secularised

Young people, who have been informed in school about how the opponents to women priests behave, are reacting against this. They react to the information they have been given, with few opportunities to evaluate what has been said; and they react honestly, believing that women are oppressed and treated as if they were unclean. Here are our allies. They do resist something they see as unfair. That is an interesting perspective, considering the institutional agenda against the dissidents. It is possible to continue with that agenda as long as people do not know what is happening – but when the power elite in the Church system is forced to refuse ordinations and block fair promotions, people will understand.

A healthy system can accept and even appreciate objections as contributions to the maintenance of the health of that system. When it no longer can do this, it is collapsing. The answer must be, not to create a ghetto, but to create a spiritual life open to the needs of the people for whom Christ died. That is a programme far removed from mere congregationalism, where the priests retreat to their parishes, but it is a programme for the reformation of the Church in a situation where bureaucrats and bishops are not willing either to listen or to understand. They do think that they are responding appropriately to the situation in a secularised welfare State. They can understand that some problems must be dealt with by modernising the organisation. The thought that they are making a fundamental error never occurs to them.

Being faithful to the secularised is to analyse what is happening in the Church and find the vision once again. That is what Martin Luther did, a confused monk and theologian hearing confessions, and understanding the needs of the people and the breakdown of a Church system.

In well-known circumstances

When St. Paul describes his mission in Miletus he stresses that he has taught in public and in the homes of the Christians. To the priests from Ephesus he gives a warning. They must keep watch over themselves and the flock which the Holy Spirit has placed under their charge. There will come men, fierce wolves, who will not spare the flock. They will come 'from your own group' (Acts 20). In public and in our homes we must understand that to be an apostolic Church means to be prepared for something more serious and more important than arranging parish festivals. It is really a matter of life and death. God gave his ministry to man for this struggle.

A Church well established in the leisure sector of the welfare society ought to be reminded of what it is really about. Perhaps God is teaching us that lesson now, when we turn from civil religion, or bourgeois religion, back to a living Christian faith: carried not by a minority, but by a remnant.

To set free the Church of England

Stephen Trott

There was news recently (May 1996) of the appointment of a
new Archbishop of Dublin, elected by a panel of bishops,
clergy and laity from the Church of Ireland. Such a simple
procedure is a refreshing contrast to the byzantine Crown
Appointments Commission which has evolved latterly in the
Church of England, masking the fact that new bishops are still
appointed by the Crown, in a procedure which dates back
directly to 1534 and Henry VIII's breach with the wider
Catholic Church.

The conflict between the interests of the State and of the
Church in England goes back a very long way. The desire of
the Crown to control or to manipulate the Church for its own
ends took a more dramatic form in the Middle Ages, when the
Church itself held considerable power and influence in the
affairs of the realm. There was constant dispute between the
Crown and the Papacy over the appointment of Bishops, who
held high office in the State as well as the Church. Such
disputes are typified by the condemnation of Archbishop
Thomas Becket at a royal council in Northampton in 1164, for
his attempts to secure greater independence for the Church.

The Church sought constantly to order its own affairs freely,
without interference by the King. The very first clause of
Magna Carta in 1215 is concerned with such matters, notably
including the question of episcopal elections without interference by either King or Pope:

> 'In the first place [we] have granted to God, and by this our
> present charter confirmed for us and our heirs for ever that

the English Church shall be free, and shall have its rights undiminished and its liberties unimpaired; and it is our will that it be thus observed; which is evident from the fact that ... we willingly and spontaneously granted and by our charter confirmed the freedom of elections which is reckoned most important and very essential to the English Church, and obtained confirmation of it from the lord pope Innocent III; the which we will observe and we wish our heirs to observe it in good faith for ever.'

The Reformation in England under Henry VIII was in some ways comparable to the process of nationalisation by modern States of major utilities within their territory which belong to private companies holding a local monopoly; or belonging to foreign companies or states whose influence is thought undesirable. Spiritual authority, which was exercised by the undivided western Catholic Church, had long been mingled with claims by the Bishop of Rome to exercise a political role, which grew increasingly unacceptable to the rulers of the emerging nation states of Northern Europe. The special status in law of the clergy, and in England their continuing right to be taxed separately from the general populace, were sources of continuing irritation to the Tudor monarchy.

The principle of *cuius regio, eius religio* ('the King decides the religion of the State') is seen very clearly in the shape taken by the English Reformation under Henry VIII. Exercising great power within his own nation, and remaining at heart a conservative Catholic, he shaped the English Church in his own likeness and image, retaining most of the essentials of its doctrine and worship, but stripping it of its independence from the Crown, and robbing it of much of its accrued wealth.

The King imposed his own version of the Catholic faith on his kingdom, in which he arrogated to himself the authority of the papacy, declaring himself in the Act of Supremacy of 1534 to be 'the only Supreme Head in earth of the Church of England called Anglicana Ecclesia.' There were to be no further appeals to Rome from the English courts, at the head of which the King himself was now placed. All jurisdiction in spiritual as well as temporal matters now derived from the Crown, rather than from the papacy.

It was the Henrician legal system which still prevailed at the start of the nineteenth century. Nevertheless, at the heart of the Oxford Movement was the notion of a Church exercising spiritual authority derived not from the State, but from the unbroken apostolic succession of the bishops and clergy. It was firmly imprinted on the minds of Anglicans of the High Church tradition, and it is still believed to be the case, that the Church of England exists by the transmission of spiritual authority through the apostolic succession. Was this not the manifesto set out by Newman in the first of the Tracts for the Times?

> 'There are some who rest their divine mission on their own unsupported assertion; others, who rest it upon their popularity; others, on their success; and others, who rest it upon their temporal distinctions. This last case has, perhaps, been too much our own; I fear we have neglected the real ground on which our authority is built, – OUR APOSTOLICAL DESCENT.
>
> 'We have been born, not of blood, nor of the will of the flesh, nor of the will of man, but of GOD. The Lord JESUS CHRIST gave His Spirit to His Apostles; they in turn laid their hands on those who should succeed them; and these again on others; and so the sacred gift has been handed down to our present Bishops, who have appointed us as their assistants, and in some sense representatives.' (*Tract I*)

This is what the Oxford Movement was about: not the revival of Gothic architecture, not about the restoration of a medieval liturgy, or vestments, or religious orders, or any of the other things which came in its wake. It was an assertion of the apostolic succession as providing spiritual authority for the Church of England to minister in this country as the local expression of the catholic Church. This spiritual authority was intended to provide a firm bulwark for doctrinal orthodoxy, against the growing liberalism in the interpretation of Holy Scripture, and in the teaching of theology in English universities; and in the face of the final dissolution of the unique privileges which the Established Church had historically enjoyed.

Inevitably such a programme had had its political consequences, which led to a degree of separation of Church and

State. This occurred especially as liturgical uniformity broke down, when at first the obsolete ecclesiastical courts proved unable to enforce the law, and latterly Parliament itself attempted unsuccessfully to hold back the Ritualist movement in 1874, by means of a Public Worship Regulation Act. The Court set up under the Act, itself a supreme example of Erastianism in the minds of contemporary High Churchmen, was further vitiated by the appointment of a prominent divorce lawyer, Lord Penzance, as its first judge. It rapidly became unworkable as clergy defied its decisions and denied its authority, and five priests went to prison for contempt of court for refusing to obey the Court's directions.

It was political opposition to Roman Catholic Emancipation in 1829, and Peel's consequent resignation as MP for Oxford University, which brought the Evangelical Newman into the High Church fold, and it became increasingly clear, even to those such as Keble with a rather Romantic idea of the Church of England, that the Establishment was finally breaking down under the influence of political change. John Keble, whose edition of the works of Hooker was published in 1836, had grown up under the influence of the last embers of the nonjuring tradition. Hooker's vision of Church and State united in one common purpose, had provided for centuries a theological apologia for the High Church tradition of an Established Church incorporating the spiritual authority of the historic episcopate.

Although the Church of England became fragmented by successive divisions and the rise of the Dissenting Churches, and the claim of the Church of England to be exclusively the Church of the English people became less and less defensible, defenders of the principle of Establishment have continued to rely upon Hooker's defence of the polity of Anglicanism. William Gladstone defended the unitary Establishment in one of his earliest works, *The State in its Relations with the Church* of 1838, a position from which he later withdrew. As Prime Minister he was personally responsible for the disestablishment of the Church of Ireland in 1868, and later gave what protection he could to the Anglo-Catholic clergy, deeply unpopular with a strongly Erastian Parliament, whose Public Worship Regulation Act was only one of many bills introduced with the aim of curbing the doctrinal and liturgical aspirations of the Ritualists.

Keble was one of the last old-fashioned High Churchmen to expound the notion of a unitary Establishment of Church and State in one common purpose, and his 1833 Assize Sermon represents a radical recognition that the old order could no longer be sustained even in theory. He observed in the Preface to the Assize Sermon that: '... the Apostolical Church in this realm is henceforth only to stand, in the eye of the State, as one sect among many, depending, for any pre-eminence she may still appear to retain, merely upon the accident of her having a strong party in the country.'

Those with ears to hear and eyes to see will recognise in the Preface remarkable parallels with much of the present day Church of England:

> 'How may they continue their communion with the Church established, (hitherto the pride and comfort of their lives,) without any taint of those Erastian Principles on which she is now avowedly to be governed? What answer can we make henceforth to the partisans of the Bishop of Rome, when they taunt us with being a mere Parliamentarian Church? And how, consistently with our present relations to the State, can even the doctrinal purity and integrity of the MOST SACRED ORDER be preserved?'

These Erastian principles had in fact been governing the Church of England for several centuries. The Convocations of Canterbury and York lost all authority when Archbishop Sheldon foolishly surrendered in 1664 the clergy's long-held and precious right to arrange their own taxation. Parliament had legislated for the Church ever since, with the Convocations permanently prorogued during most of the eighteenth century. But it was the formal ending of the unique place of the Church of England in English life which prompted the reaction from Oxford High Churchmen which became known as the Oxford Movement. Parliament, which was the legislature of the Church, had previously been open only to members of the Established Churches of the United Kingdom. Catholic Emancipation, coupled with the Reform Act of 1832, swept away the remaining ground on which Keble stood.

The Oxford Movement set out to restore the Church of England at least to the condition in which it had existed in Laud's time, to revive its vestigial claim to have maintained the apostolic succession, and to reawaken the clergy to their spiritual calling. If the concept of a unitary Establishment could no longer be maintained, then fresh emphasis must be laid on the spiritual claims of the Church of England, represented especially by its bishops and clergy. An unfortunate side-effect is that the Oxford Movement has always been very largely a clerical movement.

The conflict with the State into which this brought the second generation of High Churchmen, now called Ritualists or even Anglo-Catholics, brought about the great transformation of liturgical life which took place during the last century, and was the most important factor in the restoration of the Convocations, first as a debating chamber, and latterly in the shape of the Church Assembly. An increasingly secularised Parliament found less and less time and enthusiasm to deal with legislation for the Church, and the outcome of a Royal Commission on Ecclesiastical Discipline set up in 1904 was a recommendation that the Church should be given greater freedom in liturgical matters. An Archbishop's Committee on Church and State recommended that the old Convocations should be linked with a House of Laity to form a Church Assembly, and for the first time the Church possessed a body with the expertise and authority to legislate for itself, although under the terms of the 1919 Enabling Act, this required (and still requires) the assent of Parliament.

At the same time the Oxford Movement brought about a growing sense of the apostolic authority of the episcopate, which under the influence of men such as Edward King and Charles Gore came to act more as a college of bishops, and less like a component of the House of Lords. The rejection by Parliament of the Revised Prayer Book, in 1927 and 1928, accelerated this trend, by forcing the bishops to assert their own authority within the Church to determine such matters. The Church Assembly grew in independence and authority until in 1969 the new General Synod formally combined the Convocations with the Houses of Laity. The 1974 Worship and Doctrine Measure followed, and the process of securing a decent separation of Church and State seemed to be complete. The Church had finally obtained its freedom in almost every important aspect.

Unfortunately, it is on the very question of the episcopate that such a rosy illusion breaks down. Spiritual authority in the Catholic tradition rests, not only upon the physical expression of apostolic succession in the laying-on of hands, but also upon the handing-on of apostolic teaching. For many years following the Reformation in England, the bishops and their clergy were as much creatures of the State as of the Church, especially during the period when Parliament legislated alone for the Church. Secular opinion inevitably shaped the Church during this period, and not least its bishops, whose manner of election remained virtually unchanged, on the nomination and appointment of the Crown.

It is a salutary experience, to read through the Acts by which Henry VIII detached the Church in England from the authority of the wider Church. They are superbly written and carefully crafted, to ensure that the Crown would get its own way, in all things temporal and spiritual. They include procedures for the selection of bishops which are still in force today, despite the creation in recent times of a Crown Appointments Commission, to propose names of candidates to the monarch.

In fact, little remains of the mediaeval settlement which placed absolute power, in Church and State, in the hands of an anointed monarch, other than the procedure for nominating bishops in the Church of England. The development of a democratic Parliament and of the office of Prime Minister has eroded to vanishing point the undergirding theological justification for royal control of the Church, that of the divinely appointed Prince governing the two Kingdoms in one State. The influence of the monarch in matters of Church and State has been replaced by the influence of prevailing opinion in a secular Parliament. The Church now seeks to accommodate itself not to the religion of the King but to the less definable (but equally significant) balance of liberal opinion in a pluralistic Great Britain. This is expressed in the secular media, in the framing of statutes by a legislature which is no longer constrained by the Judaeo-Christian ethical tradition, and in the universities, from which almost all trace of their Christian origins has now been largely eradicated at the institutional level.

It is a strange irony that generations of Anglicans have looked down on their Scandinavian kinsfolk, with something of an air of pitying condescension, as belonging to State Churches with State bishops, and therefore lacking in the spiritual authority conferred by the apostolic succession which survived the Reformation, albeit miraculously, in England. Closer ties with the Lutheran State Churches in Norway, Denmark and Sweden, are proving uncomfortable for English Anglicans, for the light which they throw on our own Church soon shows up aspects of the Church of England which make it closely comparable as a State Church to its Scandinavian cousins.

Not the least of these parallels is to be found in the Swedish State Church. Although it is a Lutheran Church, and looks to the Confession of Augsburg as its doctrinal basis, it has as good a claim as the Church of England to retain apostolic succession. Moreover, the iconoclasm which characterised the Church of England in various Puritan phases has left our Church remarkably bare in comparison to the riches of mediaeval Sweden, which retained both its liturgical tradition and its ecclesiastical furnishings largely intact.

The singular difference between England and the Scandinavians is that in Scandinavia the unitary Reformation settlement actually survived intact: here, it broke up into various shades of sectarianism, dissent and free Churches. Early in the nineteenth century, our Parliament legitimised virtually every kind of religious body, and the cherished dream of an Established Church for all the people was dissolved into an ecclesiastical free-for-all. With the singular disadvantage for the Church of England, that while freedom was being bestowed on everyone else, it remained as firmly tied to the State as the Scandinavian Churches, and so was as influenced by the development of the secular State as its counterparts across the North Sea.

The first Measure passed by the Church of England Assembly did not become law until 1920. Until that time, all legislation for the Church had to be by Act of Parliament. Measures passed by the Church still continue in 1996 to be subject to Parliamentary scrutiny and veto. The General Synod proposes Measures, which are then enacted with the authority of Parliament. The Church has always had to take into consideration the likely outcome in Parliament of any proposed Measure, which may in practical terms have been beneficial in some instances, but is hardly the mark of a Church which exists as a divine institution exercising spiritual authority.

Where matters of trusteeship of money and property are concerned, all the churches other than those which are determinedly sectarian require the involvement of the national legislature in securing the protection of the State for their decisions. Disestablishment would not affect the Church of England's need to refer such matters to the State. But the question becomes acute for Catholic and Evangelical Christians, however, when the issue under consideration is of a spiritual nature. How can the charge of Erastianism be denied when ecclesiastical legislation of a spiritual nature must be ratified by a secular Parliament and by a constitutional monarch? And the problem is of a more subtle nature than simply securing assent to Church Measures.

A Church which continues in partnership with the State, even in the vestigial form which survives of the former Establishment, is not free to form its mind and to frame its life according to the Scriptures and to the teaching of the Church which is derived from the apostolic tradition. Its bishops, who continue to be appointed by the State and to sit in the House of Lords as members of a secular legislature, are inevitably still officers of State as well as servants of the Church. They can hardly keep themselves apart from the prevailing intellectual fashions and opinions of the day which flourish in a cosmopolitan body such as the House of Lords.

What is more, the experience of church government since 1919 shows that the clergy and laity who comprise the members of those two Houses are themselves faced with the same pressure, to conform to the expectations of liberal opinion in society at large, and to undervalue the distinctive doctrinal and ethical teaching of Holy Scripture and church tradition as the sources of authority for decisions made in the name of the Church by, first of all the Church Assembly, and latterly the General Synod. A Church which proclaims its

apostolicity has to find ways in practice to ensure that its legislature is conformed to the apostolic tradition.

It is right that the laity should be formally involved in the
legislative process, but unlike the clergy, members of the
House of Laity are not required to undergo any formal theological study. Again, in an age when the formal theological
qualifications of the clergy themselves have been significantly
reduced, it is a cause for particular concern that significant
sections of both Houses do not have the professional expertise
in the study of theology which would ideally be required of an
ecclesiastical legislature. Members of Parliament, it may be
argued, are not required to hold any formal qualifications; but
here we are considering the needs of the Church of England,
which professes the faith uniquely revealed in the Holy
Scriptures and set forth in the catholic creeds, which faith the
Church is called upon to proclaim afresh in each generation
(Canon C15, *Of the Declaration of Assent*).

The development of a system of church self-government,
ironically enough in view of the desire of its first proponents
such as Charles Gore or Neville Figgis that the Church should
have spiritual freedom, has actually resulted in binding the
Church more closely to the State in some respects. The synodical system is widely perceived as a system of government
which parallels that of the State, and which to a great extent
draws its authority from the State, which continues to validate
its legislation and to enforce the powers of its legal system.

At the local level, there remains a powerful desire to maintain at least the outward appearance of a continuing
Christendom in the parish system. For good theological and
pastoral reasons, both our fonts and the doors of our Churches
remain open to all comers. It is this which finally distinguishes
the Church of England from those Churches which exhibit the
characteristics of a sect. But the general perception of this situation is not so much theologically based as attributed wrongly
to the Church of England being the Established Church. We
could not continue to minister in the parish churches, it is
wrongly claimed, if we ceased to be the Established Church.

The problem with disestablishment, which has been debated
in a series of Archbishops' Commissions this century, is that
it is difficult to say what it would mean in the context of the

modern Church of England. The formal links with the State, in the appointment of our bishops, in the Parliamentary veto retained over Church Measures, and in the ecclesiastical legal system, *could* be broken, especially if a reforming government were to modify the House of Lords or to abolish it. To remove the bishops from the Upper House might precipitate a complete and formal disestablishment, in constitutional terms.

From the point of view of the Church, it would be better for the State to break the link than for the Church to be seen to repudiate the people of this country by seeking disestablishment for itself. The opportunities for evangelism and pastoral care which are afforded by the link in the public mind between the Church and the nation are at once too fragile and too valuable to risk a public relations disaster by the Church retreating behind the closed doors of half empty churches. The Church would do better to remain formally Established, while removing the remaining sources of spiritual grievance. This could be achieved by adopting the Scottish model of Establishment, in which a symbolic link with the Crown is retained, but all decisions about the Church's life and ministry are taken by the Church acting alone. In the Church of England much of this could be achieved by amending the 1919 Enabling Act to remove the Parliamentary veto over Measures passed by the General Synod.

But the far more serious matter which has to be addressed is that the synodical system has itself become an Establishment as influenced by secular models and trends as the older model of Establishment from which it was designed to set us free. The direction which the Church will take in future is strongly influenced by the perception that it is somehow to be defined by its synodical organisation rather than as a body exercising apostolic service and teaching. After all, it decides its doctrine and its policy by means of a General Synod modelled on a secular legislature, and administered by an ecclesiastical civil service. In such a context, the prevailing liberalism of the secular world has a far greater potential for influence, with the unspoken assumption that the Synod must not appear to be too far out of touch with the Parliament from which it sprang.

The Church needs to open itself up to the teaching of the Scriptures and to the prompting of the Holy Spirit, which it can not do effectively when it is fettered either to a secular Parliament or to a secularised system of Church government. Two things must finally happen if the Church is to be set free from its worldly captivity.

The first is to provide for the election of the Church's apostolic ministry by the people of God in each diocese, by means of an electoral college which chooses the bishop whom they want to be their chief pastor. It may mean the loss of representation in the House of Lords, which can on occasion be a valuable opportunity for the Church to be heard in important debates on issues of morality or justice. But the episcopate is given to the Church to build it up in faith, and the qualities sought in bishops who are to be leaders in the Church may not be the same as those required of those who must play a part in national government. The Church needs its bishops to be set free from such concerns, from the burden of administration and public engagements, to serve the Church in preaching and in pastoral care.

Secondly, the synodical system must be opened up to direct election, both in the House of Clergy and in the House of Laity. Roughly one-third of the clergy sit either ex-officio or as representatives of tiny constituencies; while the laity of the Church of England do not elect their representatives, who are chosen for them by members of Deanery Synods. The General Synod must be made far more responsive to the wishes and needs of those who constitute the Church of England, and the introduction of elections for all three Houses, of Bishops, Clergy and Laity, will go a very long way in this direction, by removing the influence of those who hold power by their office, rather than by the consent of those whom they serve.

The Church of England needs at last to rediscover the true sources of its authority to minister in the name of Christ, which lie not in the Crown, nor in Parliament, nor in its Synods. A system which is cut free from such imaginary sources of authority has a far greater chance of turning to those which really do belong to the Christian faith, in the pages of Holy Scripture and in the apostolic authority which has been handed on to its bishops to minister the Word and the Sacraments.

There remains the concern expressed above about the

competence of members of the Synod at all levels, to exercise a genuinely apostolic and spiritual judgement in all things affecting the Church of England, as they seek to order its life and to plan its mission. But if the Church were to become free, as envisaged in Magna Carta, to pursue its own life independently, and on the basis of Christian doctrine and teaching, then those who seek candidates for the episcopate, and those who elect clergy and laity to the Synod, will choose for their representatives and chief pastors those who place a high priority on the necessary skills. The level of theological awareness and expertise available to the Church can only begin to rise, once the true value of such things is appreciated once more and encouraged both in seminaries and in the theological training which ought to be made available to lay Christians.

Complete disestablishment would be no guarantee that the Church of England will become properly catholic and apostolic any more than the profoundly secularised liberal churches of North America, which have never been established. It ought not to be seen as a panacea for the liberalising of the Church of England. But reforms ought to begin which will take it several steps in the direction of a church built upon the rock of Christian doctrine and tradition, rather than the fickle bedfellow of contemporary opinion. Disestablishment may or may not prove to be the outcome, or a radically pruned version of it along Scottish lines.

The evolution of freedom for the Church of England must now take its latest course, as the raised hopes and expectations of a new millennium begin to take hold of popular feeling and sentiment. It is time for a fresh Archbishop's Commission on Church and State, designed expressly to make the Church of England more apostolic, catholic and missionary, and to shed whatever bonds from the past which hinder such a goal, in readiness for the twenty-first century.

The Language of 'Lite' Religion: Episcopacy and Apostolicity in Contemporary Anglicanism

Geoffrey Kirk

A familiar feature of the modern supermarket is the number of products which, whilst more or less accurately simulating the appearance of familiar and traditional foodstuffs – yoghurt, cheese or coffee, for example – in no way resemble them either in flavour or nutrition. They are designed, it seems, for a market of those who, on the one hand, dislike the product in question (how many drinkers of instant coffee would refuse a well made espresso?), or, on the other hand, are so incapable of regulating the quantity of food they consume that an alteration in the nutritional value of their intake is the only way to compensate for their disability.

'Lite' food is similar in concept to 'children's food'. The burgers, bangers and fish fingers which children like (or are supposed to like) are almost wholly dissociated from actual meat or fish. The protein content is low, the carbohydrate content is high, and the taste is suigeneric.

It is the thesis of this essay that the Church of England (and other churches which have recently made radical adjustments to their doctrines of the sacred ministry) are in the business of provisioning a society which has developed a distaste for the natural product, with what can only be described as 'Lite' religion: a version of Christianity which offers neither flavour nor nourishment, one which feeds neither the imagination nor the

reason. It is based on that 'lowest common denominator' principle by which we deform the taste buds of our children. For
alas, many who relish burgers, bangers and fish fingers in
formative years never graduate to cassoulet, filet mignon de
chevreuil and sole Dieppoise when the time comes.

This process of homogenisation (clearly observable in the
Anglican family of Churches, and I suspect among our
Scandinavian cousins as well), is one which involves a subtle
and ingenious manipulation of language. By a fascinating exercise of linguistic *leger de main* concepts and notions long
thought to be clear and defined are first obfuscated and then
displaced. 'Lite' religion supplants traditional doctrine, and
nowhere more so, I want to suggest, than in the understanding
of the bishop and his work.

In her study *Authority in the Church: A Challenge for
Anglicans*[1] Dr Gillian Evans makes the point that the bishop's
role is to preserve the unity of the Church at three levels. He
serves as a focus of unity within the diocese, between the
diocese and the wider church, and he symbolises continuity in
time because of his place in the apostolic succession. He
brings about this unity by his being and his teaching; by what
he is (sacramentally and functionally) and by what he causes
(and forbids) to be taught. The recent documents of the
dialogue between the Church of England and the Moravian
Church in Great Britain and Ireland put the same point more
succinctly: '... Bishops ... are representative ministers of
continuity and unity ... they have a role in relating the local
Christian community to the wider Church, and the universal
Church to their community.'[2] And the Dogmatic Constitution
on the Church of the Second Vatican Council (*Lumen Gentium*)
gives the idea more extended expression:

'That divine mission, entrusted by Christ to the apostles,
will last until the end of the world (Matt. 28.20), since the
gospel which was to be handed down by them is for all time
the source of all life for the Church. For this reason the
apostles took care to appoint successors in this hierarchi-
cally structured society... The individual bishop ... is the
visible principle and foundation of unity in his particular
church, fashioned after the model of the universal Church.

In and from such individual churches there comes into being the one and only Catholic Church. For this reason each individual bishop represents his own church, but all of them together in union with the pope, represent the entire Church joined in the bonds of peace, love and unity.'[3]

The fact is, of course, that in some but not all Churches of the Anglican Communion, the ordination of women to the priesthood and subsequently to the episcopate, has to a large extent undermined and/or negated these traditional and essential functions.

The Bishop and the Local Church

A diocese is a local expression of the universal Church, and its local unity and cohesion serves to set forward the unifying and reconciling work of Christ himself through the relationship of priests and bishop in one ministry of service. The case is very clearly put in the Dogmatic Constitution on the Church (*Lumen Gentium*) of the Second Vatican Council:

'Priests, prudent co-operators with the episcopal order, as well as its aids and instruments, are called to serve the People of God. They constitute one priesthood with their bishops, although that priesthood is composed of different functions. Associated with their bishop in a spirit of trust and generosity, priests make him present in a certain sense in the individual local congregations of the faithful, and take upon themselves as far as they are able, his duties and concerns, discharging them with daily care. As they sanctify and govern, under the bishop's authority, that part of the Lord's flock entrusted to them, they make the universal Church visible in their own locality, and lend powerful assistance to the upbuilding of the Body of Christ.... On account of this sharing in his priesthood and mission, let priests look upon the bishop as their father, and reverently obey him. And let the bishop regard his priests, who are his co-workers as his sons and friends, just as Christ called his disciples, no longer servants but friends.... Because the human race today is joining more and more into a civic, economic and social unity, it is that much more necessary that priests, united in concern and effort, under the leadership of the bishops ... wipe out every kind of division, so that the whole human race may be brought into the unity of the family of God.'[4]

The Church of England, of course, has no document which so clearly states the collegial relationship between priests and bishop in one diocese. The doctrinal minimalism which characterised its statements about the sacred ministry at the Reformation and into the seventeenth century has left its mark ('The sixteenth century documents of the Church of England concerning the ordained ministry reflect in a remarkable degree the familiar truth that in England the battle between Reformation and Counter-Reformation was not fought to the finish', the Report on The Priesthood of the Ordained Ministry,[5] comments, rather coyly). But the traditional formula used at the induction of an incumbent 'Receive the cure of souls which is both thine and mine', whilst it has no formal status as an expression of Anglican doctrine, accords reasonably with the view expressed above. And Canon A4, remaining unaltered from the canons of 1603, expresses the same notion in a rather defensive and juridical fashion:

'The Form and Manner of Making Ordaining and Consecrating of Bishops, Priests and Deacons annexed to the Book of Common Prayer, and commonly known as the Ordinal, is not repugnant to the Word of God; and those who are so made, ordained or consecrated bishops, priests, or deacons according to the said ordinal, are lawfully made, ordained or consecrated and ought to be accounted, both by themselves and others, to be truly bishops, priests, or deacons.'

Perhaps something could be made, also, of the hint in Canon C18.4 ('Every bishop is, within his diocese, the principal minister ...'). but we are in the realm of allusion and not of clarity. The minimum position of the Church of England, therefore, seems to be that all ordained persons should recognise the orders of all other ordained persons as regular and valid, and. where appropriate, equivalent to their own. A more developed position seems to acknowledge a collegial and co-operative relationship between a priest and his bishop. That might surely be taken to imply a wider collegial fellowship of all the priests so related to the same bishop.

The ordination of women to the priesthood, however, which, by internal agreement between proponents and opponents within the House of Bishops has been introduced into every diocese, has brought about a radical change. In the years immediately before the enactment of the legislation it became clear that a substantial body of opinion (perhaps a third of the whole church) would not accept the orders and legitimacy of women so ordained. Opponents of the measure, organised in a grouping called 'The Cost of Conscience', argued for the repudiation of the authority of bishops who so acted, and the regrouping of dissentient clergy around bishops in whose college of priests they could in good conscience take a part.[6] Their aim in doing so was to preserve, as far as possible in changed circumstances, the role and authority of the bishop as focus of unity and fount of order within his diocese. They proposed that the 'diocese', which had come to be seen in crudely geographical terms would return to its origins as a gathered community of bishop, clergy and people, and that each diocese should retain the necessary integrity of order and doctrine. Nothing new would be created in this development. The church already knew and accepted parallel jurisdictions;[7] and the Anglican Communion was familiar with dioceses of opposing views on the ordination of women which nevertheless co-existed in the so-called 'creative tension' of Anglican interdependence.

But it was a manner of proceeding which proved hugely unattractive to the English House of Bishops, whose attachment to the principle of territoriality above all others is probably unique among any comparable group of mammals. The bishops (who in the matter of the ordination of women are best understood as victims of their own timidity and of the ambiguity of their relationship with the General Synod) saw themselves as pressured by two not inconsiderable political forces in a battle (conducted ferociously both in the press and in the media) which was unprecedented in the life of the Church of England. The Measure upon which the vote was

eventually taken was largely the creation of the bishops themselves, as was the Act of Synod which followed and completed
it.

The two documents together might most charitably be
viewed as the sort of pragmatic compromise on which
Anglicans have not infrequently prided themselves. They
allowed women to be ordained, whilst continuing a recognised
place in the Church for those who cannot accept their ministry.
But every theological compromise is necessarily something of
an oxymoron; and few have been more oxymoronic. For by
effectively suspending the operation of Canon A4, which
demands recognition of all the Church's ordained ministry, and
upon which slender thread, as we have seen, the whole
catholic understanding of the relationship of the presbyterate
and the episcopate and their collegial function in the Church
of England depends, the Act of Synod simultaneously ensured
that neither of the warring factions would get what they
wanted. It effectively ensured that the very life of the Church
of England henceforward would be, to parody Clausewitz, war
carried on by other means: the one party continuing to seek
the parallel jurisdiction it needed, the other the women bishops
it supposed itself to have earned. Some bishops even came to
fear that the former would, after all, prove to be the price of
the latter.

The language of the Act of Synod deserves careful attention.

'1)   The Church of England through its synodical
      process has given final approval to a Measure to make
      provision for the ordination of women to the priest-
      hood.

2)   The bishop of each diocese continues as the Ordinary
      of his diocese.

3)   The General Synod regards it as desirable that
      a)   All concerned should endeavour to ensure that –
           i) discernment of the rightness or otherwise of the
           decision to ordain women to the priesthood
           should be as open a process as possible; ii) the
           highest possible degree of communion should be
           maintained within each diocese; and iii) the
           integrity of differing beliefs and positions

> concerning the ordination of women to the priest-
> hood should be mutually recognised and
> respected...
>
> b)   the practical pastoral arrangements contained in
>   this Act of Synod should have effect in each
>   diocese.'

From the prominence given it in this preamble, it will be seen
how important to those who drafted the Act was the fact that
the diocesan bishop was to remain the 'Ordinary' of his
diocese. But we need to ask what that might mean in the
altered circumstances which the ordination of women and the
Act of Synod has brought about, and whether or not it remains
a possibility.

The Measure brought before Parliament was careful to respect
the absolute rights of individual bishops to ordain whomsoever
they chose. It gave to incumbent diocesans the right not to ordain
women. This absolute right to ordain or not ordain, is of course
part of that 'proper, ordinary and immediate'[8] power of which
the Dogmatic Constitution speaks and which is required so that
the bishop can truly shepherd his flock, nourishing them with
apostolic doctrine and banishing and driving away all erroneous
and strange opinions.[9] But notice here how the meaning of the
word 'Ordinary' ('one who has of his own right and not by
special deputation immediate jurisdiction in ecclesiastical cases,
as the archbishop in a province or the bishop or bishop's deputy
in a diocese'[10]) is adjusted by the context in which it is used.

Among the many 'desirabilities' which follow is a respect
for 'differing beliefs and positions' and the notion that
women's ordination is subject to an 'open process of reception'. Effectively what this obscure example of churchspeak
actually means is that no bishop can act upon his own convictions (or on what he takes to be the doctrine and tradition of
the church universal), but is constrained to behave as though
he had no opinion (or rather as though there was as yet no reli-
able opinion to be had). It need hardly be said that there is
scarcely a bishop who now thinks as he is obliged to act. If
this is jurisdiction, then it cannot be described as 'ordinary'.
While the preamble goes out of its way to insist that the diocesan is still the Ordinary, it suggests that in a matter of

undeniable importance to his ordinary jurisdiction he should not exercise it.

But actions speak louder than words. For those who did not immediately grasp these contradictions in cold print, the Bishop of London (now Archbishop of York) obligingly played them out in dumb show. Having surrendered his undoubted right to forbid the action, he attended, in his own cathedral, the ordering of women as priests by a representative of the Archbishop of Canterbury (one of his own suffragans), himself engrossed the meanwhile in the writings of the Fathers. That the 'Ordinary' should be present at, and yet be overtly inattentive to, the very rite which characterises and defines his relationship to the college of priests in his diocese, is powerfully eloquent of the theological disruption which the ordination of women has caused and which the Act of Synod has regularised. It is a neat reversal of the rites of the Western Church for the morning of Holy Thursday. And yet, apparently, it is well within the understanding of episcopacy envisaged by the Act.

Nor is that disruption merely 'theological' (in the modern sense of 'abstruse and theoretical'). The Act of Synod incarnates it by permitting parishes, in effect (though admittedly not in theory) to reject the ministry of their diocesan in favour of a PEV, or 'Flying Bishop', whose opinion in the matter of women's ordination (and often in much else) agrees with their own.

Whatever the theory, in practice (and it is salutary to recall that Anglicanism is nothing if not pragmatic, and therefore opportunistic), such an arrangement is bound to extend itself to other areas (in many places it already has done so with regard to ordinations). It surely follows that if the authority of the diocesan can be challenged because he ordains women, the same will almost certainly prove to be the case (as events in Norway have shown) when he approves of abortion on demand or ordains practising homosexuals.

By attempting to hold together irreconcilable and incompatible opinions under the jurisdiction of one bishop the Act of Synod has effectively redefined episcopacy. Though the Act asserts that the diocesan remains the Ordinary, such can no longer be the case in any real and practical sense. Whilst

Canon A4 is suspended (by the mutual recognition and respect for 'the integrity of differing beliefs and positions' which the General Synod regards as 'desirable') and whilst those differing positions and beliefs are objectified in the existence of what is, in fact if not in theory, an alternative episcopate, the diocesan bishop is rendered dysfunctional. He exercises with regard to many in his diocese a merely juridical and largely secular role. His is the authority, not of Jesus Christ and his Apostles, but of Pontius Pilate. There has come into being a 'Lite' episcopate – one which looks like, and on occasion acts like, a true episcopate; but which can no longer be that focus of unity and fount of authority which bishops exist to be.

The bitter truth is, of course, that so long have Anglican bishops neglected their role as guardians of orthodoxy, and so infrequently has their ministry been experienced among their own clergy as one of healing and nurture, that in many quarters the change will go unnoticed. It has merely affirmed and accentuated what was the general direction and momentum of Anglican drift.

The Bishop and the Church World-wide

Englishmen of a certain age remember with nostalgia the Empire and Commonwealth tour undertaken by the present Queen immediately after her Coronation. In the days before the ubiquity of television we were marched in neat crocodiles in our school caps to watch Pathe News features at local cinemas. The young Queen was hailed and greeted by Maoris and Eskimos, head-hunters and cattle ranchers in a spectacular which proved to be the last fling of Empire.

As the century draws to its close, nearly fifty years later, those stilted camera shots and faded Pitkin Pictorial brochures seem to come from another world. Though the Commonwealth drags on, it is an institution which history has side-lined. With Quebecois separatism and Australian republicanism, even the white dominions seem set to throw off their connections with Great Britain and its Crown. The world-wide family which that tour was intended to showcase is of little significance beside the greater European trading area to which the United Kingdom is increasingly committed.

What is true of the British Commonwealth of Nations is also true, in a large degree, of its ecclesiastical shadow, the Anglican Communion. Like the Commonwealth itself the Anglican Communion is a recent invention, and like the Queen on her accession, the last two Archbishops have felt it desirable to visit it extensively (the pictures of Dr Carey being received by the native Anglicans of Papua New Guinea brought back happy memories of the fifties to many an ageing clergyman).

Paradoxically (as it now seems) the Anglican Communion both as an idea and as an institution may be said to have begun with an attempt to resolve doctrinal controversy. The Colenso Crisis in South Africa in 1863 led churchmen in North America (ironically, it now seems) to seek some forum among Anglicans in which a common mind on doctrine and discipline might be reached. The Church of England, in the person of Archbishop Tait (who, with the Bishop of London, claimed the greater part of the inhabited globe as his jurisdiction), understandably treated the approach as something of an impertinence. The resulting Lambeth Conference was first envisaged as a one-off event. The Dean of Westminster even refused to lend his Abbey for the occasion! Grudgingly it was allowed to settle down as the event of a decade. Ominously, from the very beginning, it was thought to be permissible only as long as it did (and could do) nothing.

The era of the confection and early development of the Lambeth Conference co-incided with what has been called America's 'gilded époque' or 'Age of Opulence'. It was, say Lewis, Turner and McQuillin in their book on the New York architecture of the period, 'the age of aestheticism, extravagant expenditure and the Episcopal Church'. Much of the money which created the great New York and New England houses of the period was also at the disposal of a church which had become the closest thing America has ever had to an established church: the Church of the Establishment. This was the era of All Saints Ashmont, of the megalomaniac St John the Divine, New York and of the project to overawe Washington with a great gothic cathedral (on the aptly named Mount St

Alban), the whole project surmounted by a pastiche of the Bell Harry tower at Canterbury. It is not accidental that early enthusiasm for an 'Anglican Communion' proceeded largely from this North American cultural anglo-philia, and that the idea was delivered its *coup de grâce* from the same quarter as soon as anglo-philia had fallen out of fashion.

The idea of an Anglican Communion, as we now know it, gained ground in England only as the 'wind of change' blew through the African colonies. It came to seem the logical and necessary corollary of political independence, and, with one or two notable exceptions, resulted in the creation of national churches using the boundaries of the newly created nation States. But almost before most of the Communion was off the drawing board (Central Africa 1955; Kenya 1969; Myanmar 1970; Melanesia 1975; Nigeria 1979; Korea 1993; S.E. Asia 1996) its internal decay was evident. A detached diocese (Hong Kong, in theory under the care of the Archbishop of Canterbury) after minimal consultation with the Archbishop, and after an ambiguous correspondence with the nascent Anglican Consultative Council, ordained two women to the priesthood in 1972. The action of Bishop R. O. Hall in ordaining, and the inaction of Archbishop Michael Ramsey (in failing to discipline one who, though half the world away, was clearly under his jurisdiction) opened a pathway in Anglicanism from private judgement to public policy which others were to tread.

To the dispassionate ecumenical observer it must seem strange that, though the first Lambeth Conference had foreseen just such a crisis, and had resolved to provide for it, no real progress had been made. Alas, the hundred years between the first Lambeth Conference and the ordination of women in the diocese of Hong Kong were years of lost opportunity for the development of structures and institutions to manage radical doctrinal change. The report of the Eames Commission (The Archbishop of Canterbury's Commission on Communion and Women in the Episcopate, 1988–1993) records the fact with tragic resignation: 'The first Lambeth Conference called for higher synods above the provincial level precisely for the maintenance of "Unity in Faith and Discipline" (1867, Res 4). But while this remains an aspiration, we have to live as we actually are: a communion still learning what it means to become more fully a communion.'[11]

Even after the Hong Kong ordinations no steps were taken to create inter-provincial structures to deal with what no one could doubt was an developing crisis. By the time of the 1978 Lambeth Conference women had been ordained in two other provinces (USA and New Zealand). The Conference's response was to seek tolerance and co-operation. The Lambeth Fathers were assured by Professor John Macquarrie, acting as theological adviser, that women's ordination was a 'second order issue', and so of no great consequence in the matter of communion. It was the view which was to hold sway for about ten years, and to influence the thinking of the many in a crucial period. It was not finally exploded until the publication by the House of Bishops of the Church of England of their Second Report on the Ordination of Women (GS829). The Bishops then wrote:

'It is sometimes argued that this is a "second order" question, such as obligatory clerical celibacy, not impinging on "first order questions" such as the doctrine of the Trinity, or of the person of Christ or of the Atonement, where the central tenets of the Christian faith are plainly at stake. However we have come to doubt whether in this context such a distinction is useful. This is for two reasons:

a) For many of those who favour the ordination of women, as well as for many of those who do not, the question is not one of comparative doctrinal indifference, it is seen as closely bound up with what is believed about the nature of God, about Christ and about the Church, and about creation. It is thus intimately related to the "centre" of the faith.

b) The distinction is also unhelpful insofar as it may appear to imply a distinction between matters of faith as primary and matters of order as secondary. But it is an article of faith that the Church is a communion of saints. The ordained ministry is a principal instrument given by God for the maintenance of true communion. In this way questions of Church Order touch on matters of faith.'[12]

Perhaps inevitably, in a gathering of bishops, it was the consecration of Barbara Harris to the episcopate which concentrated the collective episcopal mind. The Lambeth Conference of 1988 requested the establishment of an Archbishop's Commission to examine the problems of 'Communion and Women in the Episcopate' (for all the world as though there had been no problems raised by their ordination to the presbyterate!). The Eames Commission met for the first time in the same year and for the fifth and last time in 1993. It is not insignificant that this was precisely the period of most intense debate on the ordination of women to the priesthood in the Church of England. The Commission was clearly seen, in some quarters, as a sounding board for ideas which might come in useful if the English opponents proved intractable (as indeed they did). It issued three reports, now available under one cover from the Anglican Consultative Council.

Two principal ideas dominate the thinking of Eames.

The first is the acceptance of the status quo as somehow an expression of 'classic' or 'essential' Anglicanism. Provincial Autonomy, for example, which, as we have seen, the first Lambeth Council was called to prevent, is now taken as normative. There remains no more than a sentimental attachment to the notion that communion between bishops of the catholic church should be made of sterner stuff than this:

'While the provinces are autonomous in matters of order and discipline, they are held together by visible bonds of communion and thus in a real sense belong to one another; they are interdependent. The life of the Communion is held together in the creative tension of provincial autonomy and interdependence. The different provinces have come to a greater realisation that they need each other's spiritual, intellectual and material resources in order to fulfil their task of mission. Each province has something distinctive to offer the others, and needs them to be able to witness to Christ effectively in its own context.'[13]

It is as well to be reminded that this is not theological or ecclesiological language. It is the language of white Commonwealth politicians, nostalgic for Empire and influence, backing up their wishful thinking with offers of Third World aid. Why, if the Provinces are 'autonomous' in order and discipline, we must ask, are they not autonomous in all things else; and how long will it be before they declare themselves to be so: homosexual marriages in the diocese of Newark, New Jersey; and polygamy in parts of Africa?

Predictably, under the circumstances, the report also exalts synodical government as an essential feature of Anglican polity:

> 'As Anglicans, we value participation in synodical debate, which brings together the leadership role of bishops with the college of presbyters and deacons in decision making, as well as representatives of the whole people of God in this process. This is an important instrument in the discernment of God's will for the Church under the guidance of the Holy Spirit.'[14]

It is as well to be reminded how audacious in the defence of one novelty (provincial autonomy) is this appeal to another novelty (synodical government). Synodical government, of course, is the *engine* of provincial autonomy; but, in its present form, it can claim no greater antiquity. In England, for example, the General Synod was created in 1970. Its antecedent body, the Church Assembly, with more limited powers, dates only from 1919. It is true that consultative structures existed in the provinces of Canterbury and York from the Middle Ages, in the shape of the two Convocations. But the Convocations were not 'synods' in the sense in which the Commission is using the term. Nor did they suppose themselves to have the powers to amend and extend doctrine which the Synods of the various provinces or 'national churches' of the Anglican federation now assert. The paradox is that Anglicanism, having survived and flourished for four hundred years without synodical structures, developed them at just the moment when nineteenth century dreams of an 'Anglican Communion' were being realised in exciting and unexpected ways, and when the autonomy claimed for them was least desirable and most damaging.

Even more audaciously, the Report tries to portray its own recommendations as part of the prevailing Anglican ethos:

'If Anglicans mean what they say about "an open process of reception", such ambiguities will be accepted as one of the growing pains of living in a church where there are no binding central decision making structures. Many Anglicans will actually rejoice in this until there is a more balanced and acceptable model of universal primacy and conciliarity available ecumenically. In any case that is how Anglicanism actually is and has been since wider communion and structures were severed in the sixteenth century'.[15]

It is as well to be reminded that it was not 'Anglicans', however defined, but the authors of this report who came up with the notion that there could be a 'process of reception' for what had been presented as a *fait accompli*, and is in practice irreversible. Nor can the need for 'open reception' credibly be laid at the door of the reformers. They established no dogma-making body in the sixteenth century, not because they were patiently expecting a reformed papacy and a tailor-made Trent, but because they wanted no more dogma. Their failure to innovate doctrinally was not the sad result of lack of means; on the contrary, their deliberate choice not to create such structures was the happy result of their reluctance to innovate!

In these three instances, then, and in many others, the Commission mistakenly presents as consistent with the consensus of the Anglican past, developments which are at best deviations and at worst distortions.

The second dominant theme of the Eames documents is a predictable shift from dogma to sentiment. A single paragraph makes all plain:

'When bishops feel impelled to say that they do not recognise the orders of a minister, they should do so with charity and pastoral care, being fully cognisant of the hurt and distress that this would cause both to the ordaining bishop and the ordained person concerned. By the same token the pain of the bishop withholding recognition ought not to be underestimated. Indeed, given the sensitivities of those involved, the commission wishes to counsel prudent reticence in making public declarations of this kind, so that the highest possible degree of communion may be maintained even in this circumstance'.[16]

This paragraph, pitifully inadequate though it is, is the nub of the whole Eames endeavour. It speaks of sentiment when it should appeal to reason; substitutes good manners for sound doctrine; and seeks to make a matter of public import into one of merely private and personal concern.

The talk of 'pain' is frankly distasteful. Beside other pain – the pain of bereaved parents and of oppressed minorities – what kind of pain is this contrived ecclesial anguish? Indeed, what pain should a man feel if he experiences rejection as the consequence of his own action, freely undertaken, when he has been duly admonished that it will be unacceptable to many? Such 'pain' borders on the histrionic and should be treated as such. But 'pain' is not the main issue.

The problem is that the Commission is trying to make private what is public by its very nature. When the Commission counsels 'prudent reticence' in making public declarations about the orders of a priest it comes close to denying the very nature of orders themselves. They are not a personal possession, about the theft or denial of which someone can be legitimately pained; they are public language about relationships within the Church; the relationship of priest to bishop, of priest to priest, of bishop and priest to faithful people, and of the whole Christian community to the Christian centuries. Orders declare the intention of the contemporary Church to be faithful to the Apostolic tradition. They are therefore always a matter of public concern.

It is true that to deny someone's orders or to express grave doubts with regard to them, is a very serious matter. But it is so, first and foremost, not because of any 'pain' caused, but because of its implications for the sacramental life of the whole Christian community – beside which all faithful followers of the crucified Lord will joyfully acknowledge that their own 'pain ' and disappointment is as nothing.

World-wide Anglicanism, we may conclude, is clearly an arena in which it is very hard to be a bishop.

For reasons which are partly historical and partly temperamental the Communion seems to have rejected its own warnings about the dangers of provincial autonomy and all notion of inter-provincial synods or councils. Even in ecumenical negotiations with other groupings Anglicans have conducted their business in virtual provincial isolation (for example: the parallel negotiations between the Episcopal Church in the United States and the Evangelical Lutheran Church of America, on one side of the Atlantic, and the British Anglican Churches and Nordic and Baltic Lutheran Churches on the other. These were conducted with little or no reference to one another, and resulted in quite different conclusions about episcopacy and the apostolic ministry). The role of the Lambeth Conference, it appears, is merely to restrain provincial developments where that is still possible and warmly to endorse them when the attempt has failed. Only with Rome and Orthodoxy have discussions been international, and this in response to their catholic agenda.

All this is deeply unhelpful to a bishop who genuinely seeks to foster and embody the wider unity of the Communion beyond his own diocese and province and among all the bishops of the catholic Church. In the absence of institutions which support him in that ministry, and because of the existence of institutions (the Provincial Synods) which on occasion do the opposite, he is very much left to his own devices. Anglicans, whilst preening themselves on the size and influence of their Communion, have turned their backs on an essential element of episcopal governance. Conciliarity – the coming together of the bishops of the whole world under the guidance of the Holy Spirit to speak to the Church with the voice and authority of the apostles themselves – is not, as it must now seem even to Anglicans, an optional extra (to be invoked in times of crisis and forgotten when the crisis has passed). It is part of the very nature of the episcopate.

> 'The collegial nature of the episcopal order found expression in the very ancient practice by which bishops appointed the world over were linked with one another and with the Bishop of Rome by the bonds of unity, charity and peace; also, in conciliar assemblies which made common judgements about more profound matters in decisions reflecting the views of many.'[17]

In place of this apostolic college the Anglican Communion has substituted a ten yearly gathering of those who cannot even agree on whether all its members are bishops.

But it is not merely the failure to create the institutions of conciliarity which cripples the individual bishop in his witness to world-wide unity. The ease with which the Communion (through non-conciliar means, like the Eames Commission) comes, to accept the theological *status quo* (what one or more provinces have recently enacted) as its own defining characteristic, allows the individual bishop little or no recourse to the theological *status quo ante* (what all the provinces once had in common). In the name of the Archbishop of Canterbury and through some nebulous and recently created central quango, the world-wide Communion seems to be claiming allegiance to the contrived, over against fellowship in the received, as the heart and essence of Anglicanism.

Add to that a growing tenor of ecclesiastical emotionalism, which is inclined to prefer feelings to reason, and both to the tradition, and you have once more, the defining characteristics of a 'Lite' episcopate: one which wears (increasingly) the trappings of the middle ages, and clings to the idea of 'dioceses' and 'provinces' which it inherited from the later Roman Empire, but cannot deliver on that unity which was the Lord's charge to the apostolic college and which springs from local forbearance and world-wide collegiality.

Perhaps a 'Lite' episcopate is the design and delight of a post-modern church. Like a multi-storey carpark disguised as a Chippendale bookcase, the surface details need no longer have any reference to function or purpose.

The Bishop and the Christian Centuries

Bishop Michael Adie, on whom the lot fell to propose the legislation for the ordination of women to the priesthood in the General Synod of the Church of England, began his presentation of the case with a remarkable statement: 'The question now to be decided...is whether women, as well as being Readers and deacons, should also be priests. I put to the Synod that the answer is yes; the ordination of women to the priesthood is a reasoned development consonant with Scripture and required by tradition.'[18]

The extravagance of his claim (unnecessarily extravagant in

a Synod which was to show no vestigial interest in patristic theology) was not wasted on Alec Graham, Bishop of Newcastle (chairman of the Doctrine Commission of the Church of England).

'I have scrapped the speech which I had written.... It was the Bishop of Guildford's speech which moved me to abandon my own, for he made some points which I venture to say deserve to be questioned. He will forgive me for speaking plainly. I hope that I heard him correctly and that I quote him correctly. He stated ... that Scripture is inconclusive on the matter of the ordination of women. Surely Scripture never addresses that question? As far as I recollect that precise question is never addressed. Then he claimed that the ordination of women is consonant with Scripture. We all know that to be a matter of opinion.... Then he claimed that is was required by tradition. That really is quite a claim. He conceded that the ordination of women to the priesthood is not required by the tradition in the sense that it has never happened before, but tradition is not just doing what has been done before, an ever heavier load of practices and prohibitions. The Bishop maintained that the ordination of women to the priesthood is demanded by the truth, required by the truth, as it has been handed down to us. ... Surely it is quite misleading to enlist tradition without qualification in favour of this legislation, for it is at this very point that the arguments in favour of the legislation are at their very weakest. I hope the Synod will not be beguiled by the Bishop of Guildford in this respect, for he begs the question whether this is a legitimate development of the tradition at this stage in our Church's life. The answer to that, I submit is either "not proven" or a straight "no".'[19]

The case which Bishop Adie put, in his short opening speech, was scarcely sophisticated. He based his assertion on an particular understanding of the Incarnation and on a deliberately understated doctrine of the representative nature of priesthood:

'Our traditional and basic understanding of the Incarnation

is that in Jesus Christ, God took human nature and became embodied as a human person. He took human nature. Human nature or humanity is available in only two forms, male and female, and God, when incarnate, had to be one or the other. That does not mean that, whichever he had chosen, we would for all time have a have a one-gender ministry of the same sex as he chose. God became incarnate as a man rather than a woman, but in becoming man he took human nature which comprises both male and female. For centuries we have accepted men in the priesthood as the automatic consequence of God taking human nature, but then for centuries it was only men who enjoyed education, political leadership, the vote and so on, and these have only gradually, even grudgingly, become available to women. What God has made clear to us in our century is that women are not inferior to men, nor are they identical; men and women are complementary; together and equally they make up humanity. That simple but fundamental truth which God has shown to us in his world now resonates with a renewed understanding of the Scriptures.'[20]

This concatenation of unsupported assertions begs more questions than Alec Graham was prepared to indicate. Is the maleness of Jesus, or rather (taking due account of the omniscience and omnipotence of the Godhead) *could* the maleness of Jesus be insignificant in the way Bishop Adie assumes? What does it mean to say that women and men are equal but different; is this really an insight vouchsafed only in this century; and is a priesthood of both men and women a necessary or even appropriate way of expressing it? In what way does the priesthood derive from and refer to the Incarnation, and in what way does it represent the Lord's incarnate humanity? How would a priesthood of both women and men relate symbolically to the traditional (and profoundly biblical) understanding of the Church as a nuptial mystery? And so on.

Of course it would be absurd to have expected Adie to address all of these in the time allotted, or even to expect the Synod to have dealt with them, in appropriate depth, in the debate of a single day. What is disturbing is that a debate which began with the assertion that women's ordination was

'required by tradition' encompassed not a single citation from
the Fathers. This startling omission is to be attributed to three
main causes. The first is the general and overwhelming ignorance of patristic theology which now characterises the
Anglican clergy; the second is the prevailing (and not wholly
unrelated) superstition that the issue of women's ordination
was not squarely addressed in the patristic period; the third is
a timid sensibility that, in a mixed forum of bishops, clergy
and laity, such allusions might be thought to be tastelessly
elitist.

Whatever the reasons, the references and allusions were not
made. Nor were they any more in evidence in the discussion
documents prepared for the General Synod in the period
immediately preceding the vote. GS829 (the Bishops' Second
Report) is wholly innocent of patristic references. What the
Bishops' Report provides is a contemporary assessment of the
scriptural evidence (with little or no indication of how that
same evidence was marshalled by Christians of preceding
generations) and a narrowly opinionated assessment of current
social and demographic trends. (The one passage of scripture,
for example, which comes closest to negating the Bishop of
Newcastle's assertion that the subject is not directly addressed
in Scripture (1 Cor. 14.33bff; see Manfred Hauke, *Women in
the Priesthood?* Ignatius Press, 1988, pp.372ff.), is dealt with
by the bishops with the utmost brevity (GS829. paras. 100-
103) and apparently in ignorance of the work of Gerhard
Dautzenberg (in B. Jendorff and G. Schmalenberg (eds.)
Tradition and the Present (*Tradition und Gegenwart*) Bern and
Frankfurt, 1974)).

More disturbingly Bishop Adie's assertion that women's
ordination is required by tradition seems to be based on ignorance or misconstruction of the very patristic texts to which it
appeals. The argument from the doctrine of the Incarnation,
which is the Bishop's strong suit, was first advanced in a more
explicitly patristic form by Richard Norris, Jnr. in a paper for
The Anglican Theological Review, June 1972 (subsequently
republished in *Feminine in the Church*, ed. Monica Furlong,
1982). It is founded on conclusions drawn from arguments
advanced by St. Gregory Nazianzen in his dispute with
Apollinarius.[21] The case is very succinctly put by Daphne

Hampson in her book *Theology and Feminism:*

'In an article written in support of the ordination of women
to the priesthood in the Episcopal Church in the United
States, Richard Norris ... argues that the tenets of patristic Christology are such that it cannot be said that a
baptised woman is differently related than is a man to
Jesus as the Christ. Indeed that to say that she was, would
be fundamentally to undermine patristic Christology. The
most definitive statement to which attention may be drawn
in this regard is the much-quoted reply of Gregory
Nazianzen to Apollinarius: "What is not assumed, is not
redeemed" – or in Greek, "not taken on, not healed". The
context was Apollinarius' denial that Jesus' was a humanity like ours. Gregory argues that if God did not take on a
humanity like ours, then we are not redeemed; for it was
through sharing our humanity that Christ redeemed it. Now
if it could be said that God in Christ took on specifically
"male humanity", then women would be outside the
scheme of salvation – and that has never been suggested. If
it is to be held that both women and men find salvation in
Christ, then it must be simply "humanity" which is of
significance as having been taken on. Norris in fact claims
that in the patristic period nothing was made of Christ's
maleness, as also not for example of his Jewishness, as
being of Christological significance. Were his maleness (or
Jewishness) to be brought into play, Christ would not be
the saviour of all. Such a Christology is in no way specifically a "feminist Christology". It simply does not allow
that differences of sex, as also not of race, are of significance Christologically'.[22]

This notion probably underlies the accusations of heresy
against opponents of women priests made by Dr George Carey
not long before his translation to Canterbury. The Scottish
theologian T. F. Torrance certainly thought so, and expands
the argument thus:

'In view of this soteriological nature of the incarnation, it is
understandable and highly significant that the Augustinian
conception of man apart from woman was never employed,

to my knowledge, in any official council of the universal Church, as a theological reason for the claim that only a male human being may image or represent Christ at the altar. ... This strange pseudo-theological idea is a modern innovation evidently put forward by some rather reactionary churchmen in the nineteenth century, but has recently been revived as a convenient (although specious) argument for the exclusion of women from ordination to the Holy Ministry, and has been made to look ancient by being cast in the terms that only a man can be an icon of Christ at the altar (a misuse of 1 Cor. 11.7 which applies only to relations in the order of creation). What happens here is that an old ecclesiastical convention is being put forward quite wrongly as a theological truth or a dogma of the apostolic and catholic Church. Hence I believe that Dr George Carey, the new Archbishop of Canterbury, was quite right in his assertion that the idea that only a male can represent the Lord Jesus Christ at the Eucharist is a serious theological error. He was not declaring those churches and churchmen who reject the ordination of women because it conflicts with a convention long sanctioned by catholic tradition and canonical authority, are to be judged heretics, but asserting that it is a very grave mistake for anyone to convert such a convention, no matter how strongly enforced by catholic tradition, into a dogma or an intrinsic truth of the Christian Faith.'[23]

These two positions, strenuously stated and endlessly repeated, have taken their place among advocates of women's ordination as an unchallengeable orthodoxy. But they do not bear very close scrutiny.

It is simply not true, for example, that the maleness of Christ is regarded, by Gregory Nazianzen, or any other of the Fathers, as 'christologically insignificant'. When Gregory affirmed that 'What is not taken is not healed' he was not thereby affirming that Jesus, in the incarnation, took to himself some general, undetached, or unpredicated human nature, such as no other human being has manifested or experienced (that would, after all, have been to sell out to Apollinarius!). Instead he was acclaiming the fully human nature of the incarnation, with all its limitations and particularities, including sex. The Fathers, moreover, never make the error of associating sex with race or culture ('Jewishness'), as somehow incidental to 'true' or 'essential' humanity. They knew, quite clearly, that the one was pre-lapsarian and the other post-diluvian.

The Christological significance of the maleness of Jesus is quite simply that it guarantees that 'true' or 'essential' humanity in a way that the qualified androgyny advocated by Norris and Torrance does not and cannot. The author of the second letter to Cledonius would have been appalled at the rash statements ('We take it as axiomatic', reads one pamphlet prepared to support women's ordination in England, 'that the risen and ascended Christ has no gender') which have resulted from developments of their position.

Nor is Torrance's repudiation of the 'icon of Christ argument' any more secure. Whilst it is probably true that the phrase itself is not used in the patristic period, the idea which it expresses was alive and well from the earliest times.[24] What is more the iconoclast controversy of the eighth century raises precisely the issues of representation with which Torrance is dealing. At root the controversy between the iconoclasts and the iconodules was Christological. John Meyendorff explains the position of the Emperor Constantine Copronymos at the Council of Hieria thus:

'The painter, the Council of Hieria affirmed, when he makes an image of Christ, can paint either His humanity alone, thus separating it from the divinity, or both His humanity and His divinity. In the first case he is a Nestorian; in the second case he assumes that divinity is circumscribed by humanity, which is absurd; or that both are confused, in which case he is a Monophysite. These arguments do not lack strength and must have impressed his contemporaries, but they fail to account for the Chalcedonian affirmation that "each nature preserves its own manner of being". Obviously, even if they formally rejected Monophysitism the iconoclasts supposed that the deification of Christ's humanity suppressed its properly human individual character. They also seem to have ignored the true meaning of the hypostatic union, which implies a real distinction between nature and hypostasis. In being assumed by the hypostasis of the Logos, human nature does not merge with divinity; it retains its full identity.'[25]

John Saward is also clear that the iconoclasts shared Norris's superstition about Jesus having assumed a universal or unpredicated humanity: 'Iconoclasm's notion of an indeterminate humanity is a subtle Docetism. Universals are apprehended by the intellect; individuals are seen with the eyes. Were Christ's nature universal and not individual, He could only be "touched" by mind and thought, and his humanity would be an illusion'.[26]

Between the arguments of the eighth century iconoclasts and those of Torrance and Norris there are clear and important resemblances. Both require a notion of an indeterminate or unpredicated 'humanity'; the first affirms that, in consequence, there can be no representation of the incarnate Lord, the second that he can only properly and effectively be represented by a priesthood of both women and men. The peripheral arguments, moreover, in both ancient and modern situations, have an instructive equivalence.

Just as the Torrance/Norris view requires a priesthood of women and men, so it generates and sanctions female icons of the Saviour: the notorious Christa exhibited in St John the Divine, New York and its embroidered equivalent in Manchester Cathedral. Both opinions seem also to rely on the idea that the true icon of the Lord is neither a painted image, nor the priest at the altar, but the Blessed Sacrament itself. Such a view (apparently based on a misunderstanding of pseudo-Dionysius) was adopted at Hieria and expressed by Bishop John Austin Baker in a paper prepared for the Movement for the Ordination of Women.

The triumph of Chalcedonian Orthodoxy at the Second Council of Nicaea (787) can surely be seen as a condemnation both of the ancient iconoclasts and of the modern 'inclusivists'. The Lord's Eucharistic presence is not an icon (as the priest or the painted panel are icons) but his real presence; representations of him in his particular humanity are not merely permitted, but enjoined by the Incarnation itself, which effectively overthrows the second commandment. (The beards of icons of Christ and those of bishops and priests are not incidental to the Orthodox tradition in this matter.) To Professor Torrance's assertion that 'creaturely images in language about God have a referential, not mimetic, relation to divine realities',[27] one of the heroes of the iconodule party, St Theodore the Studite, roundly retorts that the priest acts *'mimema Christou'*,[28] the very phrase which St Thomas was to translate, using its Latin theatrical equivalent, as *'in persona Christi'*.

Theology knows of few, if any, knock-down arguments. But it is the tragedy of synodical government, as the Anglican Communion has developed and adopted it, that it makes decisions by majority votes (the majority, alas, differing from place to place and from time to time) in a way that encourages a desire for them. How wise, beside the extravagant assertion of Bishop Adie, seems the gentle intervention of Alec Graham: 'either "not proven" or a straight "no"'; and how we must now regret that we did not hear the speech that he had actually prepared.

The claim that women's ordination is 'required by tradition' (affirmed, as one must suppose it was, by the vote subsequently taken), and the failure of the Synod or of its House of Bishops to address the patristic evidence adequately or at all, is a very grave matter. The degree of theological levity thus demonstrated seriously undermines the claim of any member of that House to witness to the continuity in time which is the purpose and function of the Apostolic Succession. In recent documents designed to set forward full communion and interchangeability of ministry with the Lutheran Churches of the Nordic and Baltic region, a theology of apostolicity has been developed which frankly admits that the 'sign' of apostolic succession (the laying-on of hands by one on whom hands have been laid) is neither sufficient nor efficacious. It needs to be accompanied by (and can, on occasion be replaced by) an overarching or undergirding 'apostolicity' of the whole people of God.

There are problems for many catholic Anglicans in those documents; but I venture to suggest that they are not greater than the problems for the liberal proponents of women's ordination. How is a Church which does what the apostles and their successors for two thousand years never did (and which claims, in doing so, to be obliged and constrained by tradition) but which, in debating the matter, solemnly in its most exalted forum, never referred to the Fathers or the Councils of the Church, to establish those overarching and undergirding apostolic credentials? It may be, for all I know, that the Church of Denmark has them (Bugenhagen notwithstanding); but it must surely be doubtful if they subsist in the Church of England.

The Pope has recently stated that he supposes the Catholic Church to have no authority to ordain women. This is almost identical to the response of the Orthodox Church. It is a statement which has provoked, from within the Roman Church, a vociferous and predictable reaction. But it is not necessary for Anglicans to decide whether or not they agree with the papal affirmation in order for them to discern its ecclesiological significance. It asserts, and was presumably intended to assert, that the Church can, in the name of its own tradition and self-understanding alone, resist innovation. That right, to deny as well as to affirm in matters of fundamental doctrine, is the right of the Church Universal and of the bishops who give its universal presence a local expression. But it is hard for Anglicans to believe that it is a right to which their own bishops will ever give corporate expression. The Anglican experience is increasingly that bishops are imperious in inessentials and craven in matters of dogma. Yet an episcopate which cannot deny, as well as affirm, is one which cannot pretend to give voice in this generation to the ecumenism of the Christian centuries.

Conclusion

At the end of the nineteenth century the same impetus which had given rise to the Lambeth Conferences and to an awareness of Anglicanism as a world-wide federation of related churches also sought to draw up a schedule of doctrine which would constitute a sort of Anglican bottom-line in relation to the polity and faith of other communions. What became known as the Chicago-Lambeth Quadrilateral (from its adoption by the house of Bishops of the Protestant Episcopal Church of the United

States meeting in Chicago in 1886 and by the Lambeth Conference of 1888) upheld four main elements:

1. The Holy Scriptures of the Old and New Testaments as 'containing all things necessary to Salvation' and as being the rule and ultimate standard of Faith.
2. The Apostles' Creed, as the Baptismal symbol; and the Nicene Creed, as the sufficient statement of the Christian faith.
3. The two Sacraments ordained by Christ himself – Baptism and the Supper of the Lord – ministered with unfailing use of Christ's words of institution, and of the elements ordained by him.
4. The Historic Episcopate.

In subsequent unity negotiations with other ecclesial bodies (as the official documents invariable show) it is the fourth of these elements which has been the cause of dispute and concern. Anglicans have clung tenaciously to the 'historic episcopate', always supposing that they knew what it was, and that they had got it.

The crisis over the ordination of women to the priesthood and the episcopate has occasioned more ecclesiological introspection among Anglicans than among the Lutherans of Scandinavia for the simple reason that it has led them to question one of the pillars of their corporate sense of identity. Did they know what it was, and had they got it? *Apostolicae Curae* (which keeps its centenary in 1996) has always sapped the confidence of catholic Anglicans more than they care to admit. The corporate and individual behaviour of the Anglican episcopate in recent years has done nothing to diminish that anxiety. Provincial autonomy; the 'prophetic' actions of individual bishops on matters like women's ordination and homosexuality; the ready acceptance of mutually exclusive views of ministry and validity within one episcopal jurisdiction; these have all contrived to develop the notion of an episcopate more of form than of substance. For how long can a Church continue to claim to be catholic when its bishops are, in effect, congregationalists?

'Lite' religion is the religion of contemporary and local acquiescence. It is religion which is always looking over its own shoulder, anxious about what the world thinks of it. A 'Lite' episcopate is one which usurps the authority, but shirks the responsibilities, of a true and faithful apostolate. It exists to be a sign of unity within dioceses, between dioceses and across the centuries; but it cannot deliver what it promises.

The crisis over the ordination of women to the priesthood and episcopate has revealed fault lines in Anglican institutions which are set to widen in what promises to be an eventful theological future. A paradigm of acquiescence and assimilation has been established which can easily be adapted in other disputes. The sexual agenda, in terms of marriage, homosexuality and abortion still has a long way to run before Anglicans have 'caught up' with secular developments. We can be sure that the attempt will be made, and that the Righter Trial in the United States is merely one swallow presaging a long summer. We can also be sure that episcopacy will emerge from the process altered beyond all recognition.

Notes

1. SPCK, London, 1995.
2. GS1202, para. 34, p.22.
3. *Lumen Gentium*, paras. 20, 23
4. *Lumen Gentium*, para. 28.
5. *The Priesthood of the Ordained Ministry*, BMU, 1996, GS694, para. 89, p.57.
6. *Alternative Episcopal Oversight: The Agreed Statement* (CoC, London 1990), p.23.
7. *Eames Commission: The Official Report* (Toronto, 1994), *I*, para. 52.
8. *Lumen Gentium*, para. 27.
9. Canon C18.1.
10. OED, 'ordinary', sb I.i.
11. *Eames I*, op. cit., para. 61.
12. GS829 para. 33.
13. *Eames I*, op. cit., para. 36.
14. *Eames I*, op. cit., para. 41.
15. *Eames I*, op. cit., para. 61.
16. *Eames II*, op. cit., para. 57.
17. *Lumen Gentium*, para. 22.

18. *The Ordination of Women to the Priesthood: The Verbatim Record* (CIO, 1992), p.9.
19. op. cit., p.40f.
20. op. cit., p.10.
21. Migne, *Patrologia Graeca* XXXVII c181.
22. *Theology and Feminism* (Basil Blackwell, 1990), p.55.
23. *The Ministry of Women* (The Handsel Press, Edinburgh, 1992), pp.6–7.
24. *Inter Insigniores* (Vatican Collection Vol 2, Costello Publishing Company, New York, 1982), p.339 and note p.344.
25. John Meyendorff, *Byzantine Theology* (Mowbray, London, 1975), p.44.
26. John Saward, 'Christ our Lord and the Church in the Teaching of the Second Council of Nicaea', *Chrysostom*, Vol III (1988), n.1.
27. op. cit., p.8.
28. Migne, *Patrologia Graeca* XCIX c1188f.

Spiritual turpitude

Goran Beijer

'You are salt to the world.' So Jesus said, and so the Church has been. When the Roman empire crumbled beneath the invasion of the Germanic tribes in the fifth century, the Church, and especially the monks in their monasteries, preserved the Christian faith and carried it into the new situation. As a result Europe became a Christian continent. Where the Romans failed – in establishing their culture on the other side of the Rhine and the Danube – missionaries, many of them monks from England, did. Old pagan ways of living disappeared and people formed their lives according to the faith and ethics of the Bible. The Church became a strong moral force in society. St. Ambrose of Milan could demand that the emperor Theodosius made public penance, after he had ordered a massacre of innocent people. A similar thing happened in England after the murder of St. Thomas Becket in Canterbury Cathedral. The Germanic laws of marriage and family, where the rights of the clan were central, were replaced with Christian laws which safeguarded the individual. Medieval science was completely dominated by the Church.

Of course worldly ways of thinking and acting still existed. Now and again the Church was drawn into the politics of the world. In the fifth century theological questions mingled with the longing for freedom in countries at the fringe of the Byzantine Empire and the non-Chalcedonian Churches were born. In the same way in the Reformation period the theological critique of Rome combined with the will of kings and rulers in Northern Europe to free them from the grip of the German Emperor and the Pope as a political power. In the fourteenth century the king of France could arrange for a French cardinal to be elected Pope and force him to take up residence in Avignon. But basically the European way of life was founded on Christian ideals. There were, of course, always those who broke the laws, and, if caught, they were severely punished. With the Enlightenment things started to change. The rights of the individual, originating in the Church, were seen as more important than anything else. Man should be free to live his own life. The ideas of the Enlightenment, combined with the development of modern science, have now changed the culture of Northern Europe. The problem that is becoming more and more apparent is that the Church has surrendered. No longer are guidelines for living taken from the Bible and the tradition of the Church, but from the opinions of the day. The demand of the Lord for his Church is still to be salt to the world; but instead the established Churches have become a pale reflection of the world.

Most of the Churches of the British Isles and of the Nordic countries are national Churches. This is a development subsequent to their initial role in the countries concerned. Missionaries came, people became Christians and the countries were changed. It did not happen without a struggle – we all have martyrs from the missionary era. But Christian laws were enacted and the old pagan way of living disappeared. Bishops took part in the councils of the King, clergy were given a place in parliament. The Churches were much more closely tied to their nations after the Reformation. Being different from 'Papist' Europe strengthened the feeling of being a separate nation. In the Scandinavian countries those who became Roman Catholics were sent into exile. It was necessary even in England to be a member in good standing of the national Church in order to have the right to be involved in governmental affairs. The school curriculum made the learning of the Catechism central. In Sweden laws giving complete religious freedom were not enacted until 1951.

In the course of time these countries became democratic. It was no longer a king who had the power but the 'people' – 'All power emerges from the people' is the introductory statement in the present Swedish constitution. But what should be simply a political system has become something more. Modern democratic ideas grew out of the Enlightenment, but so did positivist philosophy and ethics. Not only the affairs of the state, but also those of daily life were now to be governed by majority opinion. Hand in hand with this development the conception of what it is to be a National Church has changed. Everything in the society is decided by the majority vote – why should it not be the same in the Church? If politics reflect the will of the people, should not the faith and the teaching of the Church do so too? A Church *for* the nation has become the Church *of* the nation.

The situation is complicated by the fact that for centuries Christianity was the only faith in our countries. This has led to the false conclusion that all kinds of spirituality are in some way Christian. Churches which used to have a moral impact came, instead, to be influenced by the opinions of the day. Establishment has contributed to this. When the Christian faith ceased to be the common religion there was an attempt to save the situation by watering down the Christian message. Controversial aspects of the Christian faith were smoothed out in an effort to continue as a 'Church for all'. Things which might offend were passed over in silence. The intention may have been honest, but the result has been disastrous – the Church has lost its identity. The Lord said that his disciples should be 'strangers in the world'; instead they have been thoroughly at home in it.

The established Church has a high estimation of man's longing for God. So it should, but at the same time it has failed to notice how modern man refuses to accept God. Man is accustomed to take decisions on his own and to exercise his vote in society. Now he feels himself competent to do so even before God. The will of God is just another opinion to be taken or left. This challenge to God is seen very clearly in the refusal to accept the conditions of Creation. There is an ongoing attempt to explore and master everything created and to use it for selfish purposes. In several areas the limits of Creation have been exceeded. The gap between the rich and poor areas of the world and environmental pollution are threatening the future of mankind.

One thing that modern man cannot accept is the fact that 'male and female he created them'. A great deal of modern ethics is built on the denial of any difference between the sexes, apart from reproductive capacity. In all other areas there should be 'equality', one of the foremost political concepts of our time. It is important to give women a fair place in society, but the aim of the politics of equality is far greater than that. Human beings should not be prisoners of Creation, but should dominate it and bend it to serve their priorities. This conviction of course can be seen in modern feminism, but not only there. It is more or less a basis for the current ideology of every political party. And it has been carried through into law. There is no longer any firm support for marriage and the family, obviously because they involve clear roles for husband, wife and children. Homosexuality should be accepted – in several Scandinavian countries there are now laws regulating homosexual 'partnerships'.

The question of the ordination of women to the priesthood is also part of this issue. It is intolerable that God should have given different missions to men and women, even within the Church. All this could have been merely the politics of a secular state. The Church is no longer in a position to prevent laws that are not in accordance with Christianity. But a Christian standard of living could have been upheld for Christians and as an alternative within society. The opposite has happened – secular ethics have been propagated as equally valid for Christians. In the same way as Christian faith has been conflated with different kinds of spirituality, what is considered to be Christian morality is variable.

Underlying all this is a concept of religion which is different from Christianity. Divinity is what man defines it to be. Nothing absolutely true can be said about spiritual matters. What one person discovers is as good as what others have found. There are those who have reached a deeper level than others. They are worth listening to and learning from, but the final word is always that of the individual. Religion is in the end a private matter, and someone's faith cannot and should not be questioned by others. This modern way of thinking has led to a situation where there are no truths, only opinions. In the area of faith there is no dogma, only feelings. Nothing absolute can be said on anything outside those matters that can be seen and touched – and even those cannot be trusted in the era of the theory of relativity. The spiritual world is even more relative, and it is considered impossible to say anything about it with authority.

True Christianity has another view of reality. Firstly there is an absolute truth behind everything. There is a God who is real in himself, not merely something created by man in his attempts to see a pattern in life. It is God who has created man, not the other way around. Secondly this God has revealed himself. God has made himself known, he is not only something you can feel. There are those who can speak with the authority of God. The Bible is not just one of many spiritual books, but the book which contains the Word of God. Faith is not sustained by opinions, but by careful listening to revelation, rooted in the Bible and interpreted in the Apostolic Tradition of the Church. This is also true when it comes to ethics. God has made his will known. He who has created everything has also given rules to live by in his Creation. The gifts of God will not be to man's good if they are not received and used in accordance with his will. Man is created in the image of God and must turn to God for guidance if he is to be what he is meant to be. Opinions of the day will most often mislead, because they are built on the will of men.

To the Christian belief that there is a revealed divine truth, Jesus is central. He is more than a man with extraordinary spiritual gifts. In the New Testament we follow the attempts of the disciples to understand who he really is. Already, during his life, the apostles could say that he was 'the Messiah, the Son of the living God', 'the Holy One of God'. After the Arian controversy the Church, meeting in Council, stated that he was 'the only-begotten Son of God ... who was made man'.

In the early twentieth century liberal theology changed this view of Jesus. Modern science made it difficult for people to believe in the miracles and in the resurrection, so Jesus was then seen as the great Teacher. His message was reduced to the Sermon on the Mount. It was clearly an attempt to 'save' Jesus. Without him Christianity would be meaningless. Even if much of what was told about him was considered to be legendary inventions of the early Church, at least his teaching on ethics was to be proclaimed.

But in the long run it is impossible to have ethics without faith. If Jesus is a legendary figure of the first century, then his teaching is equally vague, and what we have is not what Jesus may have said, but what the first Christians put on his lips. Thus Jesus is no longer of interest. What we find in the New Testament is the belief system of a Mediterranean religion of the first century. Since then mankind has developed and must move on to a modern understanding of faith. In this Jesus is seen, at best, as representing valuable spiritual experience. His person is of no interest. In Acts we are told that it was in Antioch 'that the disciples first got the name of Christians'. It was a kind of political designation – those who support Christ. What people noticed was their allegiance to a particular person. In our day we have a Church in which the role given to Christ is reduced. Everyone should feel free to interpret all his words after his own ideas. From being the One and Only in Christian faith, Jesus has become optional.

The dissolution of Christian faith in recent decades has led to a moral breakdown in the Church. The contemporary dogma is that there are no dogmas. Similarly there are no given ethics. Gert Nilsson, Professor at the Official Department for Theology of the Church of Sweden, and responsible for giving advice on ethical issues, has often stated, recently in a book, *Kristendomens etiska utmaning: The Ethical Challenge of Christianity* (Tro & Tanke, Uppsala, 1996) that there are no specific Christian ethics. He maintains that Jesus should be taken as an example, but the problem is that we have made an institution of the Church.

As with faith, ethics have been individualised. To have opinions about the behaviour of others, if one is not involved, is to question their human rights. There are no given standards. What is good for someone, as long as it is not hurting anybody else, should be considered right. There are situations when it is impossible to act without affecting others negatively. Then the good of the individual who has to make the decision is put first. There is a right to abortion on demand. (That there is another human being involved is hidden behind talk about the woman having the right to decide about her own body.) When it comes to divorce there is very little consideration of the children. Love has become something which only involves feelings, not responsibilities. The morality of the world has been allowed to become the morality of the Church as well. In the Scandinavian Churches it has for a long time been possible to have a church wedding, even if divorced. This is now also the case in England, and there are even those who perform services to end a marriage. When the law on homosexual partnerships was passed in Sweden the bishops said that a priest could pray for those in a partnership, but only in private with the two people involved. That advice has rightly been severely criticised, but a number of priests have gone beyond it and performed what in every respect is the same as a wedding ceremony. Homosexuality will clearly be the next issue where the morality of the modern world will confront traditional Christian values. In Gothenburg the bishop failed to take action against one of his priests who publicly blessed a homosexual partnership. The result was that fifty priests, supported by an unknown number of lay people, renounced his spiritual authority.

In the Church of Sweden catholic priests for different reasons did not, as in England, break with their bishops when they began to ordain women. They were trusting a 'conscience clause' which was included in the law. That was later withdrawn, and the bishops have not honoured the promise which they originally gave. Probably it would have been better for priests to have acted in the same way as those in England. But now that a break has happened, it is over the fact that Biblical teaching on homosexuality is not upheld in the Church.

The interesting thing is that, as fast as it abandons genuine Christian ethics, the Church is promoting itself as an expert on ethics. Priests are invited to business conferences to lecture. What they say seems mostly to be platitudes about honesty and kindness. The bishops make statements on issues such as wealth and poverty, peace, environmental protection, and unemployment, which are always in keeping with political correctness. Now and then a group in society, mostly business people, are criticised, but that is as it should be according to the liberal agenda. The Church says what people want to hear, and then supposes that it has a moral impact on modern life.

What we see is a Church losing its identity. The Christian faith is guided by what can be recognised by modern science. The positivist claim that there is no firm truth is accepted. Jesus is slowly disappearing from liturgy and preaching. The individualistic approach to faith and life is also accepted in the Church. The moral values of modern society are placed above Biblical ones. When 'Time' magazine reported on the decision in England to ordain women as priests their headline was 'The New Reformation'. It was noted that the issue was connected with many other ones. The magazine was right, but it is a reformation in the opposite direction to the one in the sixteenth century. At that time the Pope was criticised for not leading the Church in accordance with the Bible. The liberal 'reformation' of our time wants to cut the Church loose from its adherence to the Bible and to the Apostolic and Catholic traditions.

In a time of reformation it is necessary to choose sides. The English and Nordic Churches have always claimed to have preserved the Catholic tradition. What the modern world wants is something else, and those in power in the national Churches are adapting themselves to it. But in all these Churches there are also substantial groups which will not follow the agenda of today. Some have organised themselves into 'Free Synods'; they are all co-operating to defend and re-establish the true Christian tradition in their Churches. The established Churches of Northern Europe are probably damaged beyond repair. Those in power will lead them along liberal ways. But what is not to be despaired of is the Church of Christ in England, Sweden, Norway and elsewhere. The transition to something new will be painful and will claim its sacrifices. But there is no other way. It has happened before that small groups have won the day. What counts is not numbers or worldly power, but the truth and the strength of a living Christ. His promises are worth more than the 'hollow and delusive speculations' of this world.

Normlessness in the Church: The Church of Norway succumbs to Postmodernism

Roald Flemestad

The aim in the following essay is to analyse the present state of the Church of Norway. In my opinion, her current crisis is paradigmatic in nature, exhibiting the normlessness that ensues from the spiritual capitulation the Church has made in the confrontation with postmodernism. But before we describe the actual surrender, we have to discuss what is meant by post-modernism.

Postmodernism

The rootlessness and disorientation in present Western society is often characterised by the term 'postmodernism'. The expression is used to characterise a new cultural setting in post-industrial society when the previous vision of modernity as an unstoppable unfolding of progress is gone. On top of this, our living conditions today are so culturally fragmented that we can find no locus of authority that can set universal standards for society at large. Society is pluralistic in the sense that there is no agreement on moral standards but everywhere divisions concerning society's constitutive goods. Postmodernism tries to solve this lack of consensus on moral values by making necessity into virtue. In the absence of a consensus on moral values, meaning must be found in the realm of individualised self-realisation. In a 'me-consciousness here and now' I must try to overcome the fragmentation and ephemerality of the modern life situation. Accepting the impossibility of a commonality of norms and values, each one of us can only choose as guidance for moral action those values that express our personal convictions and sentiments. However, the inevitable consequence of this expressivism is that all moral judgements are merely expressions of preference, expressions of attitude or feeling. Emotivism has become embodied in our culture.[1] Seemingly, there exists no authoritative truth on anything.

The quest for the common good

It was not meant to be so. In the previous cultural epoch, that of modernism, one took it for granted that the world could be rationally ordered in a way that would give unity to life. Consequently, every man, although autonomous, lives under certain universal moral laws that must be obeyed. Man's ethical obligation is simply to discern by moral reasoning, accomplished by intuitions and reflections about what principles or actions are right, the moral order in life.

Thus for Rousseau, the spiritual father of the French revolution, nature is a voice within man teaching the laws of virtue. 'The common good', he wrote in 1762, arguing about the basis of the social contract, 'is everywhere evident and only requires good sense to be apprehended.'[2] Accordingly, man can diagnose and cure the ills of society with his own intellect unaided by the authority and sanctity of the past.

Likewise, Immanuel Kant, another philosophical ancestor of modernism, insisted that the moral law is what comes from within. Therefore, no conception of external order can govern moral reasoning. As it is man's responsibility to generate the moral law out of himself, it would be a crime against human nature, whose destiny lies in progress, if one age put the next age under certain unalterable set of doctrines. On the contrary, society must change as public insight progresses and proves itself by general consent. Rejecting all heteronomous authority as self-incurred immaturity, Kant declared in 1784: '*Sape aude!* Have courage to use your *own* understanding!'[3]

Thus, under the banner of Reason, the Enlightenment set out to create a society liberated from the irrational burden of feudal and religious tradition. The aspiration was no less than to find unity with the Universe in the communication with Reason. As aspects of the one and same harmony, reason, morality and freedom are essentially defined in terms of each other. When society is organised according to the principles of reason, man will find the solid platform for his pursuit of happiness. Minted in the slogans of the French Revolution – *Liberté, Egalité, Fraternité* – the Enlightenment vision of freedom and harmony in a *société rationelle* is turned into a programme for radical social change.[4]

The disillusion of Postmodernism

Two hundred years later postmodernism is the trauma when this revolutionary dream turned into the perhaps not so benign nihilism of modern post-industrial society. Where modernism assumed that the world could be rationally ordered in a way that would give only one moral answer to any question, postmodernism abstains from the possibility of representing the world in a unified rational and moral perspective. The chaotic patterns of modern life produce identities that are constantly changing. The shifting patterns of contemporary civilisation impose a fundamental relativism that denies reason the right to claim that only one perspective is the true and universal answer to a given moral or societal problem.

However, if the truth of assertions depends upon the perspective from which they are seen, this multiple perspective seemingly abandons the idea of man as a rational agent. There is no fixed nature of things and no truth in correspondence, no linguistic picture and no literary imitation for any inquiry to discover or decode.[5] Under such conditions, a consciousness of subjectivity does not mean a turning to a rational self, set against the arbitrary whims of life. A new understanding of the personality as a mere collage of images in the flux of time challenges the ideals of self-responsible reason and freedom, upheld by an essential self. What started in the Enlightenment as the unconditioned character of the moral self, rooted in a transcendent order of values, is in postmodernism becoming 'decentring' subjectivity lost in a contingent world without overarching meaning.[6]

But if reason is dethroned is this way, then the claim of the freedom of the self also amounts to little more than randomness. Freedom is simply, in the words of the postmodernist Richard Rorty, 'the recognition of contingency'. This means that freedom is not man's dignity to act in accordance with the moral order but the insight that the notion of 'absolute validity' is obsolete metaphysics.[7]

What is truth?

Thus, in the age of postmodernism we must console ourselves with 'relative truths' borrowing bits and pieces of insights from whatever source is available and constructing views that are useful or desirable in a given situation. But, left with a notion of truth that cannot be supplied with 'philosophical foundations',[8] we must ask ourselves: If there is no commonly recognised standard for meaning and morality, how are we then to resolve the differences among men?

Clearly there is no obvious way. Universalism must be discarded. Rather than command universal norms as given moral obligations one must allow room for private projects expressing individual self-creation. As for universal ethics, the most we can aspire to is to find solutions which can ease the societal tensions in our time in order to pave the way for the next epoch.

This calls for a communicative reason where 'truth' is simply another word for 'what comes to be believed in the course of free and open encounters'.[9] But if truth is simply the honorific title assumed by the argument which got the upper hand in the war of competing persuasions, this means that the standards for what is right or wrong must also be sought in the deliberating process itself. There is no universal standard. Only when a consensus is established among those involved can common action be taken on the premise of voluntary association.

Proceduralist ethics

A redefinition of truth from epistemology to tension-easing dialogue implies that all authority must be legitimated from below, being generated by the communicative process itself. As a synonym for individual and social progress, truth emerges in the social context and the accepted procedures for problem-solving. As a matter of fact, the parliamentarian system delivers a model for searching for truth. In a situation where one acknowledges the futility of continued confrontation, legislation by majority rule is a regulating compromise between group interests.

Of course, a proceduralist approach to what is good and right requires the agenda-setter to define, to a large extent, the premises of the discussion and thereby the outcome. For quite some time we have seen how civil society is transformed by pressure groups which by different means try to attract sympathy to their arguments for a change. Their method is to first gain public attention by presenting themselves as a minority subjected to injustice by society at large. Then they sustain their emancipatory claims using an ahistorical 'rights' language which rejects traditional morality as a form of discrimination against their just quest for self-actualisation. To give one example, agenda-setters have managed to make abortion an issue about discrimination against women by skilfully defining arguments against it as male oppression revealing a lack of tolerance and progressiveness.

However, the understanding of 'rights' as one's self-actualisation over against the traditions embedded in an oppressive society, must not be mistaken for increasing liberty or antinomian individualism. The paradoxical result of this new understanding of the modern individual as a free-floating bundle of rights, is that the sphere of liberty is continually confined as a growing number of compromises is established in order to comply with victorious interest-groups. For when they are first established, these hard won settlements command subordination in the name of the political procedures that led to them. As in the parliamentary process, the losing party is expected to acquiesce in the victorious opinion.

From the view-point of traditional morality it is all the more troublesome when partisan issues are raised to the level of 'human rights' as legal bodies, national or international, put their names behind the process. Having gained this legal status, the ethical issue turned political will re-emerge as an ethical one but now in the name of democracy.[10]

The challenge to the Church

Of course, this new consensus ethics is very different from traditional Christian ethics where the norms of what is a right or wrong action are legitimised in the Will of God to all mankind. Such an understanding of a divine order in life is very much the alternative to the notion that the so-called good and right are in the end nothing but honorific titles assumed by the claims of victorious pressure groups.

But when, as we have seen, the notion of a 'philosophical truth' and the corresponding vision of a 'universal standard' are substituted in society at large with a new political ethic of self-realisation, the Christian Church finds herself in a confrontational situation if she tries to maintain the old ways of normative discourse on theological issues.

For the Protestant Churches in Northern Europe this challenge takes a new twist because they are state Churches. In the 'good old times' this meant that the Church could call upon the State to impose Christian life styles in society at large. Today the situation is actually inverted. The State is using its political control of the Church not only to impose the new ethical insights upon the faithful but is even demanding that the state Churches give a religious validation of the new 'rights'. At least in the Scandinavian countries, we have seen since the 1950s a not-so-subtle politicisation of theology over the question of ordination of women to the priesthood being defined as a women's rights issue.

However, for the moment a new political demand is put on the Church's agenda as a consequence of current settlements of tensions in civil society. The new issue is the question of church acceptance of registered same sex cohabitation. We will focus on the articulation of this issue in the Church of Norway as an example of how the very church structure appears to collapse in the antagonism between a traditional understanding of Christian ethical norms and the postmodern conception of ethical life as individual self-realisation.

The debate in the Bishops' conference

The question of homosexual partnership was put upon the bishops' agenda in 1995 as a consequence of a radical change in family law in Norwegian society. In 1993 Parliament passed legislation equating registered homosexual cohabitation with marriage. Forced to take into account this development the bishops were obliged to take a stance on the question of the integration of same-sex cohabitants in church life, and above all to decide if they were to be ordained. All the bishops expressed their welcome at the communion table of non-celibate homosexuals living in a committed relationship; a minority of three bishops said yes to ordination but the majority of eight voted against it.

The published arguments[11] behind the conclusions fully explore the various circumstances leading up to the vote. Our interest, however, concerns the overriding moral issues: How, in the confrontation between the traditional and the new sexual ethics, is one to locate a commonality of belief in the Church, and what is the locus of authority in the issue?

The minority view

In their introductory remarks the three minority bishops state that although the biblical texts concerning homosexuality are not unimportant, they cannot carry the burden of the ethical reasoning. Over against these texts stand not only the Biblical command of love but a Lutheran understanding of Holy Scripture. A Lutheran use of the Bible in ethical questions rests on the presupposition that 'both isolated passages from the Bible and theological/ethical systems stand or fall according to the criterion of whether they lead to Christ.' This is particularly because 'Luther has taught us that the Bible contains the Word of God and is not automatically identical with the Word of God.' On this hermeneutical basis the minority bishops then warn against 'construing from a logical combination of Scriptural passages an ethical system that in practice becomes merciless.'

As a group, continue the three bishops, homosexuals live under greater strain than heterosexuals. The very fact that they cannot 'live in accordance with their identity means that they are unfree and exposed to psychic stress.' Therefore, 'the Church must find ways to promote openness and counteract the feeling of shame in the search for sexual identity.'

The Church must recognise this without prescribing norms of conduct. The minority bishops declare: 'Whatever the attitude towards same-sex cohabitation, the Church must attach great importance to promoting respect for those who out of deep Christian conviction choose homosexual cohabitation.' In practice this means that the Church must help the homosexual to 'say yes to his (or her) sexuality.' If the homosexual is obliged to live chastely, 'this would make it impossible (for him) to experience himself as a whole human being.'

Proclaiming self-realisation as the highest ethical value in this way the minority bishops refer the whole issue to the private sphere and conclude: 'The question of whether homosexual cohabitation is sin, cannot be answered. In any case, same-sex cohabitation which is upheld by fidelity and love has moral qualities of a genuine Christian character.'

Thus, it is difficult to avoid the conclusion that what the minority really means is that if the actual norms of sexual ethics are felt to be too demanding, the Biblical command must be given up. The rules of morality must be justified as being those rules that a non-celibate homosexual living in a committed relationship can be expected to accept. Therefore, in judging same-sex cohabitation, the Church cannot state the moral imperative as being a requirement to submit to the Biblical norms as an expression of the will of God.

The majority view

In a similar vein, the majority finds it 'essential that the Church manages to give room to the homosexual experience of pain ... and rebellion.' The eight bishops state that 'there is no reason to doubt that same-sex cohabitation is founded upon responsible decisions. ... Moreover there are, in this kind of relationship, human qualities which correspond to ethical values.' Thus the majority appears to recognise same sex-cohabitation as an acceptable expression of human love.

However, these bishops are quick to add that 'the Church cannot in principle open up to ethical pluralism.' The majority will not accept that the right to self-realisation is above the norm derived from the word of God. Therefore, 'when one speaks of respect for the choices made by the individual, this [respect] cannot cancel the responsibility to measure this choice against the Biblical norm of cohabitation.'

So although the eight bishops retain the principle, by thus acknowledging the practice they are saying that practice is what counts. They do not presuppose a Biblical norm that heteronomously imposes its authority; it is rather the individual who measures his own ethical choice in relation to the Biblical ideal to see how far he accepts the ordinance. The majority argues further: 'The Church must openly show respect for those who, from a genuine Christian conviction, make other choices than that which the Church recommends. ... In spite of [the fact] that they transgress the ethical instruction of the Church, they have the right to claim ... [the right to be met with] understanding by the Christian community. They must be integrated into the life of the parishes.'

However, at one point the majority bishops surprisingly put their foot down: 'The requirement of respect for other people's [ethical] choice and the will to integrate into church life homosexuals [in cohabitation] ... is not to say that [registered] same-sex cohabitants are welcome to be hired for church positions with kerygmatic ... or liturgical functions.'

In this way the majority bishops perform an inelegant balancing act. On the one hand, they embrace the idea of Christian ethics as individual self-actualisation and give up the notion of commonality of belief. On the other hand, they want to reject ethical pluralism, and this rejection is marked symbolically by the refusal to ordain same-sex cohabitants. In other words, they cannot represent the Church in public. It is difficult to avoid the conclusion that the eight bishops simply are concerned that the official façade of the Church should be left intact. Privately, however, one can do as one likes.

Mutual respect in things indifferent

This highly inconsequential argument simply reflects the overriding priority of the majority: no normative conclusion must be drawn in the name of theology. Rather, theological concepts are juggled in the air in an effort to create a functional compromise between acceptance in practice and opposition in theory to homosexual cohabitation. In this way the issue can be kept open for further discussion and compromise. It is essential, underlines the majority, 'that the theological and ecclesial discourse on same-sex cohabitation takes place in a way which secures openness and the possibility of factual disagreement.'

On this basis the majority and the minority can welcome each other. In a common postscript the whole episcopal Conference gives the assurance: 'The debate and the disagreement have not diminished the respect we have for each other. In future we will continue in the community of ministry we share as bishops of the same Church. It is our explicit wish that the issue [of same-sex cohabitation] must not split the Church. Discord and disunity must not overshadow the main thing: the Gospel of the crucified and resurrected Christ.'

With these pious words the issue is settled as a question of *adiaphora* – 'things indifferent.' Absorbed by the bishops' mutual respect, the discord will not entail any practical consequence. The whole question is really nothing but a matter for discussion.

Easing of tension in the Church Assembly

Nevertheless, fearing that the call for unity may not be enough, the majority bishops cautiously ended their deliberation by 'assuming that the statement [from the Bishops' Conference on homosexuality] ought to be sent to the Church Assembly.'

Clearly, this seemingly innocent invitation is dramatic in its consequences. It simply means that the Church, if necessary, must fall back upon a parliamentarian procedure to solve internal tension articulated by theological conflict. In clear words the request implies that the Christian community, as a mirror of society at large, has no given normative standard to appeal to, but must retreat to the regulating force of a proceduralist method to solve the struggle between unresolved and irreconcilable paradigms.

The bishops' foresight turned out to be well founded as the hope of solving the issue solely by academic discussion was not to last long. Within days of the publication of the statement from the Bishops' Conference, a dean declared himself out of communion with a bishop who had sided with the minority. Soon some fifteen priests and parish councils acted likewise vis-à-vis the minority.

In these strained circumstances the Church Assembly was forced to address the issue in the autumn of 1995. The resolution passed was Solomonic. Briefly, it was decided, on the one hand, that same-sex cohabitants were not to be ordained. On the other hand, the issue is to be put on the agenda again in 1997. Further, the question of sexual, same gender relationships was declared non-divisive so that no immediate sanction was to be imposed upon those who had declared themselves out of communion with their bishops.

Evidently, this very political compromise is a not so subtle effort to evade the core problem and bid for time. Circumventing a theological stance on the moral issue, the Church Assembly plays for time to make room for the ordination of homosexual cohabitants after 1997.

The ecclesiastical institution seen in a sociological perspective

But by treating the question of homosexual cohabitation in this way the Bishops' Conference and the Church Assembly have done more than fail to uphold the Christian answer to an ethical question. The real calamity is that in order to ease the tension the issue has generated in the Church, resolutions have been passed that make ethical judgements entirely arbitrary. There is no authoritative way left of talking about obligations which transcend the self, and about the prerequisites of moral community. Institutionally the Church refuses to give clear ethical guidance on an issue so explicitly articulated both in the Bible and in the Church's ethical teaching. Faced with the conflicting, incoherent voices of the official Church it is up to the individual to make up his or her mind about what one feels to be the right thing to do in any given situation. This retreat to moral expressivism is the self-liquidation of the Christian community, a prescription for the institutional collapse of the Church.

An institution is more than a simple mirror of social forces. In the social sciences[12] an institution is defined as a 'formal machinery' for the application of rules defining concordant behaviour in certain situations. Institutions consist of a pattern of norms, and patterns for collective orders, transmitted in a meaningful structure. Expressing patterns of interaction, the institution gives conformity to norms or consistency within a frame of reference. Thus by establishing an interpretative order in the form of institutionalised actions, tradition is legitimated and the complexity of the world is simplified for the individuals in the meaningful structure.

However, each institution has to be understood and interpreted from its own particular position. Its formation and structure, in terms of meaning, have to be cemented into the structure of the life-world of an actual society. As a pattern of collective order the institution consists of norms which are commonly shared in a collectivity or community. Seen from the aspect of consolidated conformity to rules, institutions have their roots in communal traditions and become the 'carrier' of the latter by maintaining the orders that are socially defined in the community. On the other hand, the traditional definitions of reality which are embodied in the organisation and upheld by the collectivity in mutual attachment and solidarity, come under great pressure when the validity of institutional patterns and symbols are questioned.

Anomie in the Church

The weakening of a discipline originating in and guaranteed by society is called *anomie*. Normlessness occurs when there is an acute disjunction between the cultural norms and the socially structured capacities of the members of the group to act in accord with them. In a general sense, *anomie* means the absence of a system of values or of behaviour patterns which would otherwise impose itself with authority.[13] Postmodernism is, of course, *anomie* raised to the level of philosophical doctrine. The challenge to the Bishops' Conference, and to a lesser extent the Church Assembly, was to maintain the traditional understanding of Christian sexual ethics by imposing their authority over against the contemporary view that the ethical imperative for all of us is simply to be true to one's chosen life plan. But instead of using their office to defend doctrine, they gave themselves the task of mediating between a traditional Christian ethic of ultimate ends and a modest ethic of responsible commitment corresponding to the modern idea of self-realisation.

This willingness to compromise is no innocent matter. The bishops' failure to comply with widely recognised Christian norms immediately undermined their credibility in society at large. However, because the bishops used their authority to impose an implicit rejection of traditional definitions of Christian sexual ethics and legitimated the new relativism by reference to the Bible and significant words in the Lutheran confessional tradition, the harm done to the church is simply enormous. With no authoritative, binding doctrine of human sexuality, the faithful are left disorientated as alternative normative patterns are accepted calling for behaviour and attitudes which the original definition of Christian reality precluded. The ensuing pluralisation of Christian ethics brings into question the facticity of the Christian world-view. The freedom acknowledged to belong to the individual to choose his or her version of a 'Christian' ethic, implies that 'God' is but a honorific name for his personified ideals.

A Church without identity

Since 1995 there have been no centrally transmitted symbols in the Church of Norway which inspire compliance with Biblical norms. By embracing new narcissistic norms of sexual behaviour in the name of the Bible and church doctrine, the Church of Norway will, of course, lose the spiritual heritage which served as the normative foundation of parish life. There is no turning back to the heteronomous authorities which during the centuries served as sources for Christian piety. In other words, the door is left wide open to postmodernism.

Postmodernism swims in the fragmentary and chaotic currents of change as if that is all that there is. The experience of the transitoriness of things abandons the sense of historical continuity and memory so that any meaning has to be discovered and defined from within the maelstrom of change. If the historically given is embraced, it is as irreverent pastiche and with a playfulness that undermines all metaphysical solemnities.[14] In this situation the Church will simply perish if we too lose the sense of the supernatural.

However, the way back to a unified morality in a Christian community is difficult and precarious in a cultural climate where social change and modern forms of mass communication are constantly transforming our civilisation. It is in my opinion more than doubtful that the Church of Norway, after a century of compliance with secular society, will have the resilience to resist the forces of postmodernism. The realignment of the Church presupposes a break with the present 'system' and its Erastian leadership. It is unthinkable that the restoration of the Church will take place through a leadership which dares not protect the faithful against the errors that pervade the culture in which we live, by giving authoritative guidance in the name of God. In order to overcome the normlessness of postmodernism the immediate necessity is to rediscover the lost heteronomous authorities of Christian discourse and life.

The Church as an 'interpretative community'

Firstly, this can be done by a renewal of the Christian spiritual heritage. Modernism set out in the name of reason and progress to liberate society from the burden of religious tradition. Similarly, postmodernism breaks with the past in the name of individual self-fulfilment. In both cases individual autonomy is won by the loss of wholeness.

In this situation, the challenge to the Christian Church is to overcome the vacuum by building a bridge to the sources we are rapidly losing. Such a rediscovery of the Christian tradition is not to be confused with nostalgia for a presumed golden age of theological coherence and ethical certainty. The quest is to regain the lost sense of Christian identity in order to meet the questions of the day.

On the basis of such an historical horizon and the effect of continuity such a perspective generates, the Church can again emerge as an 'interpretative community'. This sociological expression denotes a group operating within a particular institutional context where the collectivity produces particular forms of knowledge. From such knowledge interpretative communities are able to function as 'loci of resistance to domination.'[15] They function as countercultures by simply holding to what they consider to be valid knowledge and practice in opposition to society at large.

Of course, the Christian Church has always understood herself to be such an interpretative community, a pneumatic locus of resistance to 'the rulers of this age' (1 Cor. 2.8f.) and the 'God of this age' (2 Cor. 4.4) 'pulling down strongholds, as we pull down philosophies and every exalted thing that lifts itself up against the knowledge of God, leading every thought into captivity and obedience to Christ' (2 Cor. 10.4ff.). Similarly, the challenge to the traditional Christian today is to resist the world by upholding the faith given to the apostles, written down in Holy Scripture and transmitted to us through the ages by the catholicity of the Church.

Notes

1. See Alasdair MacIntyre, *After Virtue: A Study in Moral Theory* (London, 1992), p.22ff.
2. J.-J. Rousseau, *Du Contrat Social* (1762) Book IV, chapter 1. My translation. 'The evidence of the common good entails that those – Catholics and Jews – who insist on following their own revealed truths, must be banished from the state because of their

intolerance and insubordination to national religion.' Book IV, chapter 8.

3. Immanuel Kant, 'An Answer to the question: "What is Enlightenment?"' in *Kant's Political Writings*, ed. Hans Reiss (Cambridge, 1985), pp.54ff. It is Kant's particular concern that a society of clergymen must not be allowed to be in a position of guardianship over society and thus make progress in enlightenment impossible.

4. See Alan Touraine, *Critique de la modernité* (Paris, 1992), pp.24, 39.

5. See Richard Rorty, *Consequences of Pragmatism* (Minneapolis, 1982), pp.164, 198f.

6. See the philosophical discussions of societal change in Charles Taylor, *Sources of the Self* (Cambridge, 1992), pp.465ff.

7. See Richard Rorty, *Contingency, irony and solidarity* (New York, 1991), pp.46f. *et passim*. Rorty states that the notion of 'absolute validity would be confined to everyday platitudes ... and the like; the sort of beliefs nobody wants to argue about because they are neither controversial nor central to anyone's sense of who she is or what she lives for'.

8. See Rorty, op. cit., p.52.

9. Rorty, op. cit., p.68.

10. The embellishment of political issues in ethical robes was well put by a state secretary of the present Norwegian Government, who declared to the press that acceptance of same-sex cohabitation expressed 'the Government's ethics'. See *Vaart Land* of May 29th 1996.

11. The statements are published *in extenso* in the newspapers *Dagen* of April 8th 1995 and *Vaart Land* of April 10th 1995. My translation.

12. See Peter L. Berger and Thomas Luckmann, *The Social Construction of Reality* (Garden City New York, 1967), pp.116ff.; James G. March and Johan P. Olsen, 'The New Institutionalism: Organizational Factors in Political Life', in *The American Political Sciences Review*, Vol. 78, 1984, pp.734ff.; P. Münch, 'Parsonian Theory Today', in *Social Theory Today*, ed. Anthony Giddens and Jonathan H. Turner (Cambridge, 1987), pp.131ff.

13. See Raymond Arons' discussion of this Durkheimian concept in *Progress and Disillusion* (New York, 1968), pp.153ff.

14. For further elaboration, see David Harvey, *The Condition of Postmodernity* (Cambridge and Oxford, 1989).

15. See Harvey, op. cit., p.47.

The Rediscovery of Belief

Folke Olofsson

Christian belief is not a conceptual religious machine, conceived, projected and constructed in order to meet certain human needs or fulfil various human aspirations. Nor is it an intellectual structure erected in accordance with a set of criteria endorsed by a certain age or a particular group of people. Christian belief is not a construction that may be deconstructed and reconstructed, but rather a discovery of something already given. As life is something given, which precedes any human action and exists as the prerequisite condition for any human activity, Christian belief is a discovery of the works and words of the Holy Trinity. And as life is known by being lived, so Christian belief is known by living in this discovery. Christian belief is based on facts of Life. The Christian Church is one of these facts.

The Church always finds herself in the danger area between a barren traditionalism and a flimsy trendiness. The Church has a tradition, something which has been handed over to her once and for all, and which has to be handed over uncorrupted to each new generation. Tradition literally means *that which has been handed over*. But tradition is not a deep-frozen merchandise to be handled in an unbroken chain of freezers. Tradition is something living to be given afresh to each new generation, and once taken over, it is formed and coloured by the people of that time, their concepts, questions, problems and needs.

Traditionalism stands for permanence and unchangeability. The traditional is *semper idem*, always the same. In an ever-changing world there is at least one archimedic point: tradition. Of old is has been like this, and so it shall be for ever. *Gimme that ole time religion – it's good enough for me.*

Here is security, but it may be bought at the cost of irrelevance: an incomprehensible religious idiom, a liturgy that no-one any longer understands, symbols that do not speak to anyone any more. So much is invested in the past that the present never gets a chance. The Christian faith becomes a fossil and a relic. There is traditionalism in a bad sense, one that is near to death, characterised by rigidity and petrifaction.

Trendiness arises when sensitivity to all the contemporary whispers and calls is cultivated to the extent that the signals from 'the faith which has been once and for all entrusted to the saints' is no longer heard or is consistently misinterpreted. The ambition to be relevant and in tune with the times is purchased at the price of becoming deaf to tradition: the substance dissolves and identity fades away. What remains is surfing on the waves of contemporary fads and trends, all the bad copies and the ever prevailing opportunism. What the world outside the Church has long since left behind for new waves and winds, the straggling Church takes up with drums beating and trumpets sounding. So the Church becomes the sum and substance of self-conceited officiousness. Everyone who has seen the cartoon showing a knock-kneed cleric as an ice hockey goal keeper with the balloon: 'Dear lads, who is serving?', is once and for all cured from all ingratiating trend-surfing. He who marries the *zeitgeist* will before long become a widower.

The history of the Church is a continuum, a flow through history. In every instant there is confrontation between the past and the future in the present. The tension between tradition and renewal, rigid perseverance resulting in irrelevance, indiscriminate listening ending in loss of identity, has followed the Church through the centuries. And, yet, the Church still lives. Why?

Tradition has no doubt always been questioned. Objections have always been abundant: tradition is obsolete, outworn, useless. Who needs a quill pen when there is the computer? Why should we take over an antiquated understanding of the world or an outmoded view of life? We know more about human existence than any generation before us. Look at technology! Look at transistors and transplants! Look at videos and virtual reality! We now live in a new world with new values and new views. Old answers simply do not apply. Convincing as this may seem, it is not true because human life remains essentially the same throughout history. Therefore it is not appropriate to compare quill pens to a computer and apply this comparison to the warp of life. There is a *humanum* which for all and for ever remains the same: a birth-giving womb and an open grave define the room in which all theological statements take place. There is a common human experience of birth and death, joy and suffering, meetings and farewells, toothache and orgasm: all this which has been the same within and between people through the ages; all that can be told, transmitted, communicated in talks, speeches, novels, poetry, drama, tales, sagas, myths, pictures, music, and dance.

There is something given which can be handed over both when it pertains to the existential, common experience of the *humanum*, and to Christian belief. There is a substance that does not change. There is an identity which remains the same. But at the same time, there is a growth in humankind: new experiences, new questions, new answers colour and form the *traditum*, that which is transmitted. Here lies the difficulty: the meeting between that which is old, given, and that which is new, reflecting its age. The ideal is and remains a continuity which preserves the tradition uncorrupted, but makes it flow on enriched – *non nova, sed nove* – not new things but in a new way. In this sense, good traditionalism certainly exists.

The Church has no other access to the ordinary human experience of the *humanum*. This is one side of the Church, her earthly, created, human side. But the remarkable thing about the Church is that she is, at the same time, the bearer of an experience, which has been given as a gift from the outside, and thus transcends herself as the receiver of this gift. This gift is the divine revelation. The Church exists because the God who created heaven and earth, all things visible and invisible, also created the Church as a sign of God's intervention and presence in the world, the Church being not only a sign but also at the same time the mediatrix of this divine action and presence here and now.

What we call *humanum* has a divine sanction because it is created. Through his Word, God has created man and woman in his image in order to attain to his likeness. God also blessed man and woman, and even if human existence is marred by the consequences of the Fall, God has never retracted his original blessing. God the Creator has also manifested a total commitment to, and solidarity with, his creation by becoming man in Jesus Christ: The Word was made flesh and lived among us. For us men and for our salvation he came down from heaven and was incarnate by the Holy Spirit of the Virgin Mary and *became man*. Therefore, the *humanum* has a double attestation: through creation and incarnation.

In the Church the encounter between the human and the divine takes place in a visible and tangible manner. In Christ the Church has an experience of what it means to be human, which cannot be found elsewhere. In the Church the meeting between the past and the future takes place harmoniously in Christ. As the divine Word he is the One in Whom all things were created, he is the Logos structure of all creation, he is the Last by whom all will be judged and the Ultimate towards whom all things tend. In Jesus Christ the Church is already perfected. This is one side of the Church: her essential side. In one sense the Church is already One, Holy, Catholic and Apostolic.

However there is also another side of the Church: the one in time and space. Placed in time and space the Church is always only one generation away from possible extinction, balancing over the abyss between traditionalism and trendiness, petrified irrelevance and total loss of substance and identity. The religious, intellectual, moral and social environment in which the Church finds herself today is characterised by secularisation, which means that everything is measured and judged against the values and views of this *saeculum*. This presents a tremendous challenge to the Church, but this challenge is not greater than those which once confronted the Church in the past. The Church has always had to encounter the voices and whisperings of the times, the lures and threats of the age, but her prime obligation and call have remained unaltered to this day, that is to withstand the temptations and fence off the dangers of compromising her integrity through various forms of servility to contemporary projects. It would be disastrous for the mission of the Church to mankind if she lost her catholic identity by compromising it for some contemporary syncretism. In every time and age, the Church has in a sense to struggle in order to become what she essentially is: One, Holy, Catholic and Apostolic.

The mountain, the sea, the desert are settings that divest man of all his outer props and decorations and make him encounter himself in his existential nakedness. Not the mountain that can be reached by a cable car, not the sea seen from the deck of a cruising ship, not the desert peeped at from some comfortable resort, but the mountain peak reached after hours of laborious lonely climbing, the vastness of the sea experienced from a tiny sailing boat, the desert extending as far as the eye can see – they all leave man standing before the ultimate limits of his existence and reveal his existential situation: in the centre and yet reduced almost to nothing.

Man is exposed to forces over which he has no control and which at every instant may threaten to destroy him. Death is as near as life. Man is a little speck, hardly visible, and, yet, he is there, experiencing being in all its complexity. He is alive. He lives. In these extreme situations man has the ecstatic experience of the nearness and intensity of being and of nothingness, of living and of death. 'I *am*! I *am alive*! The world *is* there! And I *know it is*!' But this intense feeling of life and vitality is instantly threatened by the harrowing insight 'The world is going to be there, but not seen by me, as *I know I shall not be there.*' Man is seeing himself and his existence no longer from his own perspective but from the outside, from the horizon which surrounds him. He has seen himself in a new way as if he had been seen by another. Man has experienced something infinitely greater than his own life and existence.

To be surrounded by the horizon and to experience that one has been seen – even as if it were only by oneself – this remarkable experience of total nearness and ultimate distance is the beginning of a transcendental experience. Man finds himself standing before something numinous, which evokes in him a primordial shudder, and out of his depths breaks forth the ecstasy of being. Out of his depths also rises the horror of nothingness. And in the contrast between the experience of being and of nothingness grows an intuition: there is something unutterable, unspeakable which *is*, something which *confers being* and *stands against nothingness*.

Someone who has this experience – and people have had it in all ages – can learn how this intuition of something 'greater', 'higher', 'deeper' manifests itself in a 'thou'. This experience, however, is ambiguous and even contradictory. Man feels as if there were a possibility of contact, even communion, with this 'thou'. At the same time man also becomes acutely aware of the fact that there exists an unbridgeable gap, an infinite distance between himself, the world in which he lives, and this 'thou'. The world for man seems to be both transparent and opaque, open and closed. Man cannot escape from the ambiguity of his own existence: nothingness, despair, distance on the one hand and intuition, longing and hope on the other.

Has not the prophet Isaiah put into words the longing of humankind when he prophesies:

'Oh that thou wouldest rend the heavens, that thou wouldest come down, that the mountains might flow down at thy presence, as when the melting fire burneth, the fire causeth the water to boil, to make thy name known to thine adversaries, that the nation may tremble at thy presence! When thou didst terrible things which we looked not for, thou camest down, the mountains flowed down at thy presence. For since the beginning of the world men have not heard, nor perceived by the ear, neither hath the eye seen, O God, beside thee, what he hath prepared for him that waiteth for him. Thou meetest him that rejoiceth and worketh righteousness' (Isa. 64.1–5a).

That which in Isaiah's prophecy is a passionate longing and an ardent prayer has been fulfilled in the Christian belief. The Incarnation, God becoming man in Christ, God in the flesh, is the answer to our yearning. The divine address, the divine action, takes shape in a Visitation, in a young woman's yes, in a pregnancy, in a male baby. This is the great miracle of the Christian belief. The gulf between the human and the divine has been bridged. No longer does there exist an unbridgable chasm between time and eternity, finite and infinite, material and spiritual. The yearning and the intuition of man transcending his limited existence is met by one Person of the eternal Godhead entering into time and space. God is meeting man by being born into the world he himself has created, thereby subjecting himself to its boundaries and limitations. In Jesus Christ heaven and earth, uncreated and created, God and man, meet and unite.

Reflecting on the significance of the Incarnation the Church sees a pattern for the Christian understanding of life as a whole. All that is created, all that is human, is in one sense already sanctified through the assumption of humanity by Christ, by his life, his passion and death, his resurrection and by his returning to Father as the glorified One. All that is created, is already perfected in the presence of God. If Christ could come to a particular people at a particular time, and this particularity was an integral part of the Incarnation as contrasted with some abstract idea, a kind of gnosis which never becomes incarnated in a particular person at a particular time in history, then the Christian belief can encounter people just where they are in the very circumstances in which they live. The contingency of the human, the cultural and the historical conditions is the raw material in and through which the Christian belief is incarnated and takes shape. Traditions, customs, concepts and ideas can become integrated parts of the whole. The Christian belief has been inculturised: that is, it has entered into the cultures it has met, christened them and incorporated them into the Church.

Inculturisation is a consequence of the Incarnation and the basic sacramental view of life which flows from it. Some of the most beautiful flowers of Christianity have grown out of this flower bed. But something which in itself is good and wonderful can be misused. This has also happened to inculturisation. It has been used as an alibi for a never-accomplished conversion or change of heart and mind. Things have been 'christened' that cannot in any sense be compatible with the Christian belief. There is a limit which cannot be passed when it comes to what can be taken over and incorporated.

The mountain peak, the vastness of the sea, the desolate desert are settings which reveal man's nature and position in this world. There, man can learn a lot about himself, about the world and even about God, but certainly not all. In order for man to attain to a true self-knowledge and an adequate understanding of his existence, he needs the divine revelation which puts him in God's perspective. This perspective meets man in the icon. Here, the spiritual world looks at man and not the other way around. Man's perspective is once and for all reversed. God's perspective of man also encounters him in God's Word as the Bible reveals how God looks upon man. The divine revelation in the Bible portrays man as created in the image of God in order to attain to his likeness. Therefore there is always a longing for God in man. Man for ever bears the hallmark of his Maker.

But the biblical revelation also tells a story about man who wants to become *like God without God*, and who because of this rebellion against God is driven away from him. In his attempt to be like God, man forfeits his place in Paradise. In the crucifixion at Golgotha man accomplishes what he began in the Fall – by killing God, man finally becomes what he originally intended to be: an atheist. Man is the contradictory creature who is both yearning for God and killing him. Thus, man's existential situation cannot only be determined by his own experiences of transcendence. The Word of God has to reveal to him that he is not only a seeker of God but a sinner against God. Through his rebellion against God, the source of being and life, and the transgressions of his will, the way to perfection, man has become a slave under sin walking on a path leading away from the final goal which God has set for him. As a transgressor of God's will, man does not live in a new freedom but is heading for destruction on his way towards nothingness, which he dreads, while he is at the same time being corrupted by developing crookedly, being *incurvatus in se* instead of being open to God and his fellow man.

That which is created and human is not immediately fit to be united with the divine. All that is, exists under the conditions and consequences of the Fall, being contaminated and marred by sin. Inculturisation – the Church meeting the world – cannot be based on the Incarnation alone. It has to pass through Golgotha and the atonement at the Cross. In Christ alone the *humanum* exists in its pure and sinless form. It does not exist in the world. In Christ, however, creation, human nature and the human condition can be atoned for, reconciled, purified, sanctified and consummated. A Church who wants to retain her integrity and identity, therefore, asks how that which is created and human is lived and manifested *in Christ*. At the same time the Church marvels when she perceives how Jesus Christ is wondrously manifested in and through her, because it is *through, with* and *in Christ* that the Church receives her true and abiding identity.

The word *project* in a sense reveals its own time. A project is something man pursues from his perspective. Out of himself man projects into time and space his thoughts, and dreams, and hopes: his ideology.

The *modern project* may be used as a shorthand term for secularisation, characterised as it is by its lack of transcendence, its anthropocentricity and its attendant rationalistic reductionism, together with the sole transcendence it can accept, that of time: the future in which perfection is to be found, that is to say, Utopia. The modern project is throughout pervaded by perspectivism. There are no truths and no absolutes. All depends on from which perspective, or in whose perspective, things are seen.

The modern project has been shaken to its foundations. Its positivistic scientism does not any longer reign over the intellectual rostrum. That the modern project is on the retreat can also clearly be seen in the compromise and collapse of utopian socialism, which is one of its most inevitable and spectacular embodiments and manifestations, and of which the fall of the Berlin Wall is the spectacular and definitive emblem.

Secularisation alone does not characterise our time. In the postmodern era various and different modes of thought and sentiments of life meet and exist side by side. The world is no longer a closed box. A new awareness of transcendence is clearly to be discerned. Everywhere there seem to be signs of a new spiritual awareness and new attitudes to life which have left rationalism and atheism far behind. There is a new openness to new worlds and values.

Religion and spirituality are on their way back, not in the form of traditional historical religions, however, but rather as an eclectic amalgam of elements taken from different sources: ideologies, religions, esotericism, occultism etc. The term attached to this multifaceted and in many respects contradictory contemporary phenomenon is *New Age*. Whereas secularisation confined its perspective to this *saeculum* and to what can be measured in time and space solely by man's senses, this perspective literally opens up a new age: a novel understanding of reality, of knowledge, of man. Yet, in both perspectives the individual stands at the centre. In the religious and ideological supermarket of New Age man strolls, the consumer who fills his trolley with merchandise according to his preferences and taste: religion on private, individual terms.

The crucial question facing the Church today and which she eventually has to answer, is whether the modern project to which the Church for so long has addressed herself at the risk of losing her identity, is about to be superseded by *the syncretistic project*.

If this is the case, and everything speaks for it being so, the Church is confronted with a tremendous challenge. The Church may, of course, go on surfing on the trendy waves of modernity, and in the end become a mausoleum of recent fads and fashions. The Church may let herself be influenced and even dominated by this syncretism, which is in one sense the heir of theological modernism: religion as the creation of the human spirit or as man's reaction to the eternal mystery of life, the evolutionary, dynamic, inclusive religion. With the mystic experience or the gnostic pattern serving as the ultimate criterion for Christian belief, or for that which is understood to be the genuine Christian faith as it is defined by American and Continental university theologians, this religion will easily mix with all the prevailing contemporary elements. A religion of the new age in cyberspace and virtual reality.

The programme of this syncretistic project can be described in this way: the unknowable and unfathomable mystery of life may be expressed and manifested in various ways, and this has also happened in the great traditional religions. But now we have reached the stage in the evolution of man at which we can disregard external dividing dogmas and doctrinal opinions and unite in a knowledge, a *gnosis*, which is the common denominator *behind, beyond, beneath* all words and concepts in the historical religions with their rites and beliefs, a knowledge that is embedded deep inside every human being, only waiting to be awakened.

The syncretistic project involves an attempt to combine

elements or fragments of Christian faith with non-Christian ideas, beliefs or manifestations. The gnostic pattern of a knowledge behind, beyond, beneath, which is common to all religions, in some cases already functions as a unifying and uniting factor. Characteristic of the syncretistic project is the search for and the creation of a universal religion.

The Christian Church, however, has a deeper calling than that of pursuing either the modern project or of carrying out the syncretistic project. Its deepest calling is to realise the catholic synthesis.

The Christian faith is trinitarian. God is one God, but when the Church speaks of her experience of the One in whom she believes, the Church finds herself talking about the Father and Creator, the Son and the Saviour, the Spirit and the Sanctifier, because of the way this One God has revealed himself. The God who revealed his name to Moses at the burning bush as *I am the One I am* has made himself known as the God who is *one* God and, yet, *a communion of 'persons'*. In the modern project trinitarian belief was discarded as impossible and illogical. In the syncretistic project the traditional belief in the Trinity is reinterpreted in a way which will match contemporary demands and expectations. For the catholic synthesis it is of crucial importance that the traditional trinitarian belief of the Church remains intact, is deepened and is not distorted, as the Trinity is its ground and ultimate reference.

The Church is the sacramental means God is using to achieve the ultimate goal of his creation. The catholicity of the Church certainly has many dimensions, but the essence of her catholicity lies in her relation to the Trinity: the Creator of heaven and earth, of all things visible and invisible. The Church is the work and creation of the triune God and as such she is God's people, the Body of Christ, the Temple of the Spirit. It is the call of the Church to be catholic, encompassing the totality of God's creation.

The Church may be understood as a symbol, an instrument, an icon, a sacrament, but more than anything else as a communion. In and through the Church all that is created is restored to its full integrity and revealed in this entire potentiality: to be united with the divine in a sacramental way, of which the Incarnation is the ground and pattern, on its way towards the final goal, which is the transfiguration and consummation of all creation. The catholic synthesis has as its ground and goal the Holy Trinity: the Creator, the Redeemer, the Lifegiver; the Father, the Son and the Spirit.

All that exists is not there by chance. For the Christian all that is, is created, because God through his Word *let there be* has called it into being. All that is, is, because God has willed it to be there. Therefore the Christian has a basic trust in creation. A Christian dares to believe that there is a correspondence between God and man, between the divine and the human. Man's thirst for God is caused by God himself in order that he may quench it. Also, there is a correspondence between man's intellect and the Intellect that once created all there is and in this very moment sustains it. Delving into the depths of creation through reason in order to learn to know its secrets, and in this way attaining to an intuition of a Supreme Reason and seeing a Creator behind it, is entirely in line with the Christian belief: a boundless optimism together with a realistic insight into the grandeur of creation and the limitations of human power.

A Christian has a basic trust in creation and its order. God does not cheat. The fundamental attitude towards life is *trust the basic design*. The fact that there is an enemy which Jesus calls evil, which threatens and destroys this order, cannot upset this basic trust. When a Christian encounters evil both in the form of moral evil, that is evil which people do, and non-moral evil, that is evil which happens to people which is not their fault, e.g. illness and natural disasters, he reacts with sorrow and wrath. That is Jesus' own reaction against evil. A Christian passionately in love with creation, finding joy in it and feeling an awe for life, has the right to rage against the evil that people do, and the evil manifested in Horton's headache, Huntingdon's chorea, VACTERL-syndrome and other afflictions that man has to live with. Originally, it was not meant to be so. There is a usurper and destroyer of God's good creation. God does not want it to be this way. A Christian may hope and believe this, not as a gullible daydream escaping from a grim reality, but rather as a prophecy and a real hope that all things in the end will be well, when God's will finally has prevailed.

Everybody knows from his experience that creation in its beauty and frailty is broken and fractured. Yet there is so much beauty and wonder in life that even a severely handicapped man, who is only able to communicate through his word machine by blowing into a mouthpiece, writes: 'I don't want help today; I want help to live!' The call and task of the Christian is that of offering all creation to God in order to let Christ encompass it in his sacrifice and perfect it through his resurrection, saved, healed, cleansed. The eucharist displays what it is all about. A High Mass on a Harvest Thanksgiving Day provides a glorious illustration.

The sanctuary abounds with all that fields and gardens have yielded: golden corn sheaves, well scrubbed root crops and vegetables, dazzling flowers and mellow fruits and berries, mingled with products from local industries and factories. There are files documenting well handled commissions, business contracts of transactions benefiting both seller and buyer, stands for plastic bags with intravenous drips from the hospitals, journals of surgery, rolls of cash register receipts, diskettes containing manuscripts of novels, scientific articles, calculations of the strength of bridges, blueprints for houses, children's paintings and drawings from schools and nurseries – all that man has made and been the steward of can be brought to the altar and represented by bread and wine in the offertory.

In every eucharist the Christian congregation carries bread and wine to the altar, *fruits of the earth and work of human hands* representing the whole creation. This offering is embedded in prayer, intercession, thanksgiving and praise. The bread and wine offered at the altar are united with the word of Christ according to his institution and become a sacrament. The Word comes to the elements and a sacrament is called into existence. Christ takes up into himself all that which the Church has brought to the altar and he bears it in his sacrifice before his Father. The whole creation in its brokenness and sinfulness Christ brings in his sacrifice which has taken place *once and for all* and, yet, is for ever present in every celebration. When the priest elevates the paten the transfigured bread anticipates the transformation of all creation in Christ for which the Church longs and prays. When the chalice is triumphantly lifted up the wine is anticipatedly transfigured into the new creation without evil, sin, suffering, which all creation in birthpangs groans for. Already in this *saeculum*, marked as it is by death and decay, the life forces of the world to come break in. The calling of the Church is that of being a bearer carrying the creation in an offertory to God in Christ in the hope of a final transfiguration. The calling of the Church is that of giving the dying world a living hope and making it visible, tangible and edible.

In this process of praise and hope every individual and the Church as a whole is engaged. The process of dying and rising with Christ which has been initiated in baptism for every Christian is intensified and accelerated in the eucharist. Every communicant who approaches the altar in order to receive Christ under the forms of bread and wine has repented of his or her sin, confessed and received forgiveness. Evil has lost ground in the world in this person, and God has reclaimed another part of his creation. The eucharist is a meal which gives the forgiveness of sins, because Christ is truly present and bestows the fruits of his death at Golgotha: forgiveness and annihilation of sins. The eucharist is the anticipation of what will happen in the end when the will of God reigns.

The eucharist is concrete. When bread and wine have been united with the word of God they are not put on display in a gilded showcase beyond the reach of the congregation. The sacrament does not remain on the altar only to be looked at. The priest as an icon and representative of Christ gives it back to the people to be eaten and drunk. *Trust the basic design!* Man has to eat in order to live. Which fundamental function of life does God choose in order to come as close to us as our own hearts? God meets us in eating and in drinking, the very acts that keep us alive. God comes as spiritual food for the new man he has created in Christ. In order to become like God, man in Paradise ate what God had forbidden. Now, in his love God in the eucharist gives himself as food and drink in order to make man what God intended him to be: like God, in total communion with him.

What a *sacramentum*, what a mystery! Ordinary unleavened bread baked from ordinary wheat flour, ground in ordinary mills, sown and harvested by ordinary people – *fruits from the earth and work of human hands*. The world is sanctified through this bread and wine, as is all creation. Walking on this earth is walking on holy ground. This is the Christian understanding. The world in itself is not divine and shall not be revered or worshipped as the Mother Earth mystics propose. There is, however, a deep element of truth in this New Age mysticism. Creation is sanctified, because bread and wine can become bearers of Christ's full and total presence in the eucharist, as he was totally and fully present as both God and man in the one person of Christ. A Christian who receives the Lord Jesus in the form of blessed bread and wine longs with every cell in his body, with his whole being, for the final defeat of God's enemy and for the liberation and ultimate transfiguration of all creation.

Christian faith is sacramental because it is incarnational: the assumption of humanity, the uniting of divine nature and human nature *without confusion, without change, without division, without separation* in Christ is the ground and the pattern. Christian belief cannot but take the creation seriously because of the Incarnation. Therefore, humanity given in creation and assumed in the Incarnation, in all its various and variegated forms and manifestations, is what is fundamentally common to all human beings. This is the common ground for all human fellowship, humanism and humanity. There is a common *humanum* which applies irrespective of the conditions of time, place and culture: the instant when the pain loosens its grip, the joy of cutting the umbilical cord of the first born, the grief when the hand of the dead cools in the hand of one still living. All that is a common experience of the human condition, which one life is far too short to exhaust, and yet fills every life to the brim. There is a *humanum* because all men are created in the image of God in order to attain to his likeness, and because of the fact that all that there is, is God's creation. And even to those who do not believe in God or understand life, the world and humanity as something created, still the *humanum* remains for all people in all times a fundamental, recognisable and intersubjectively verifiable experience, common to all mankind.

The great task and call of the Church in the world is that of bringing together all that is truly human in its immense richness, manifoldedness and variety, and to bring it to Christ. As the grains of corn have been harvested from various fields, have been ground and baked into one bread, so people from all times and from all corners of the world will be united under Christ in his kingdom. Unique individuals who share a common humanity will be brought together as the Bride of Christ. Everyone will bring his gifts and riches into this cosmic wedding feast. All forms, all colours, all combinations, all in and under one Christ, who is great enough (Col. 1.15-20) to encompass all that is truly human, being the one after whose image man is created. Jesus Christ is God's image, and man is the image of the Image.

Jesus Christ is the prototype for creation and the first-perfected example of the new creation. In and through Jesus humanity becomes truly human because his human nature has its ground and being in God himself. Man was meant to be like Christ, and in the end, this is the way it is going to be.

The basic Christian attitude towards creation is one of love for all created beings, a joy at all there is and a profound respect for life. Evil and suffering are not denied, but taken up in Christ's suffering, in his atoning and healing sacrifice. With Christ as prototype and pattern the Christian is called to lead a life of service, self giving and sacrifice: being a bread for others. As Christ's arms are stretched out on the cross, so the arms of the Christian are open and stretched out to the world. But there is one great difference: the hands of the Christian are not pierced and nailed to the cross. In Christ the pardoned and released sinner can with open arms embrace life in a jubilant thankfulness and joy. As a human being man belongs to God's creation. Man is at home in God's world. 'I am Christian and nothing human is alien to me; all belongs to me and I belong to Christ.'

Christian life is lived in the world but cannot exist without the Church. The Church is the Risen Christ as he is present in the world after his resurrection and into whose body the Christian is incorporated through baptism. In the Church all barriers of race, sex, social standing, cultural background and level of education are overcome. There is a basic God-given equality between man and woman, and there is also a God-given variety of roles and functions in the Church and in the family. There is room for all the various instruments in the divine symphony. This is the catholic vision which in every age has to be presented and vindicated anew in its entire width, breadth and depth. The catholic vision and the catholic synthesis are not alien to the Church; they belong to its essence.

Christian life is a life lived in the time after Easter and Whitsuntide: *in Christ and in the Spirit*. It is lived in total openness towards God's creation in a total worldliness. The world as God has created it, redeemed it and sanctified it through the Son and the Spirit, is not to be left, despised or denied. It is to be loved, served and borne back to God to whom it rightly belongs and in whom it is already perfected.

Yet the world is too small for the Church as it is for man. Time and space cannot hold the Church or man. The perfection of life will not be accomplished in a future Utopia but in a consummation which breaks all barriers of man's limited being and imagination. The perfection of man's life lies in a communion and union with God in the eternal life, for which man has no adequate words. The Orthodox Churches call this *theosis*, deification. New Age religiosity, which even in its name tries to imitate the age to come, may open one's eyes to possibilities and stir up a longing in man by presenting shadow images. But the reality, the Body, is Christ. In Christ man has his union with God and the consummation of life. The glorified Christ already sits at the right hand of God the Father almighty, and thence he shall come again in glory to judge the living and the dead, establishing his eternal kingdom. Already Christ is now that which man is going to be. In him, in his resurrected and glorified Body, the whole creation is proleptically transfigured and consummated.

The catholic synthesis encompasses all that God has created and transcends all limits of time and space. It commences at the creation and is perfected in the life of the world to come: the new aeon. When at last God is all in all, the catholic synthesis will be finally accomplished.

The New Ecumenism:
A Way Forward?

John Broadhurst

The question facing traditionalist Christians in the present situation is how they are to progress what they believe to be their true vocation. Christendom is in a turmoil, and it has been frequently suggested that a realignment of Christianity is taking place. Orthodox members of many churches have found themselves cast in the model of victims with little hope of survival. Is it possible for these Christians to turn the situation in a way which advances the claims of the Gospel and the search for genuine Christian unity?

The State churches of Northern Europe have an establishment mentality, and surprisingly this mentality is mirrored in those unestablished churches around the world which find their origins in Europe. Establishments are by their nature adaptive, exerting great pressure on their members to conform to a pattern and style of life that ensures an untroubled future for the institution. The prophetic or the headstrong are generally ignored for senior posts, and the institution adopts a managerial style of life. Over recent decades this pattern can be quite clearly detected in many Christian churches around the world. Whether appointments are by election or selection, the tendency is for those who offend least to gain preferment. Whether they have the ability for the task, or more importantly the vision for a contemporary world, hardly enters into the debate. It is my belief that all establishments, whether political or ecclesiastical, are guided ultimately by only one principle – their survival. They deal with opposition or dissension by attempting to suppress it. Committed pressure by groups such as the Movement for the Ordination of Women, or

the Gay Christian Movement, is at first resisted, then patron-
ised, and finally accepted and promoted. Even those who do
not share a movement's aims and vision ultimately support it
because it has been become part of the establishment
programme. It is very easy to detect this process taking place
in any of the churches referred to in this book.

If this analysis is correct, then it does suggest a plan of
action for orthodox Christians. If they exert systematic and
sustained pressure for a return to traditional faith and order,
they will ultimately succeed. Many in the establishment share
their perceptions but the corporate life of the church keeps
them quiet. An institution which believes in survival as its
basic impulse, will by its nature, once it has resisted an
attempt to change it, rapidly adapt to any new pressure.

The future has to be one which returns our churches to the
orthodox faith and practice of the Catholic Church. At the
Reformation the reformers intended such a process, but their
attempt was made with partial knowledge of the early church
and against the turbulent background of the society which had
seen the arrival of the printing press. This put a vernacular
Bible in the hands of people who were often ill-equipped to
deal with it. Very rapidly a large number of competing and
mutually exclusive Christian groups and philosophies emerged,
and many of these form the bases of the denominations which
are now found throughout the world.

The commitment to Christian unity found its impulse in the
isolation of the Lutheran and Anglican Churches of Northwest
Europe – allied with the real problem of different churches
competing in a missionary situation. The basic premise, often
unstated, behind all ecumenism is that there is an inner core
of Christian faith and practice which should be common to all
Christians. This core of Christian doctrine is particularly
found in the undivided Church. Any look at the history of its
first thousand years will reveal that there is, in spite of the
complexities of early church history, an unbroken thread
running from the time of the Apostles to the Great Schism.

In recent years, ecumenism has taken a new turn. The Lima
Document issued by the World Council of Churches seeks to
find common beliefs and practices amongst Christians, establishing norms and building upon them. The difficulty with this

process is that often what it is dealing with are little more than the distortions of schism or separation. The only genuine way that Christians can come together is by stepping beyond and behind their denominational foundation documents. These documents, though of great historical importance, can have the effect of seriously distorting debate. An illustration of this is a conference which I recently attended in Scandinavia. All the participants except me were Lutherans. They were discussing the contemporary problems of the Church. Almost every speaker mentioned the Augsburg Confession. I pointed out that I had attended similar discussions on identical issues in England and America amongst Anglicans and stated that it must be inappropriate even to attempt to use their separate doctrinal statements as a base for what were common problems. The Confession, rather than clarifying, had the effect of distorting the debate and lowering the horizon.

Discussions between the Roman Catholic Church and the Anglican Communion focused on major theological issues separating these churches and came to something of a common mind. However, when the debate returned to the Church of England, many sought to criticise it using Anglican formularies created during the Reformation crisis. The initial process was common faith from scripture and tradition addressed to local problems and concerns. The response was often local historical documents used as the only authoritative base to criticise the attempt. Members of separated churches often talk and act as if the Christian revelation began in the sixteenth century.

The basic premise underlying all ecumenical attempts is that a process of convergence is a possibility. The present reality is that there is a process of divergence taking place both between churches and within them. To give one example, when the Church of England proposed to take the novel step of ordaining women to the priesthood Pope John Paul II wrote to the Archbishop of Canterbury saying it would constitute a new and grave barrier to unity, the leader of the Orthodox Church taking a similar line. They were ignored! What Christians do is more important than what they say. Is it possible for orthodox Christians in these Churches to survive and pursue a meaningful ecumenism that advances the Gospel and offers a hope of being part of a re-alignment of Christianity? If the answer to that question is negative then it would be better for orthodox Christians to seek a new home immediately.

Survival

The first issue is survival. If orthodox Christians, and the Truth, are to survive it is necessary that they stand away from the liberal majority, but only as far as is necessary for them to survive. This standing apart must be with a heavy heart; but we cannot continue acting as if nothing has happened in a Church which proclaims falsehood, denies truth, and makes the sacraments doubtful questions rather than signs of the kingdom. Christianity is an incarnational religion. It is a grave problem for orthodox Christians unconvinced that women can be ordained to the priesthood, when the Church incarnates an error by ordaining women. A similar problem arises when the Church discards Biblical ethics or the Bishops allow one of their fellows to deny basic Christian belief. A question that has to be asked is how far orthodox Christians are willing to go in the defence of Truth.

In the early Church the Fathers established the principle that orthodox Christians should gather around the nearest orthodox Bishop. In the Church of England several Bishops have privately stated that they have supported what they do not really believe in. Few hold to the old beliefs. As none of the Bishops of the State Churches are willing to come to the defence of orthodox Christians outside their own dioceses this puts traditionalists in a problematic situation. In England Forward in Faith has published a *Statement on Communion* which sets the limits of their relationship with the majority as a consequence of the majority's actions.

The statement starts from the minimal premise that there is doubt about the acceptability of women priests. It spells out the consequence of this doubt which destroys the collegial nature of the Presbyterate and breaks the relationship with the Bishop. How can a Priest act on behalf of a Bishop who ordains women and acts collegially with them? The statement suggests that to continue to do so is to affirm that which is denied. It therefore accepts the *juridical* authority of the diocesan Bishop, but not his *episcope* over word or sacrament. He has ceased in a real sense to be the pastor. In the document traditionalists set out the basis of their continued participation within the State Church and Communion with each other. It publicly recognises the real impairment of Communion which is now a reality. This could solve the immediate problem but does not offer any future. Without Bishops orthodox Christians will be exterminated within a generation. The ministry has to be secured.

The Swedish response has been copied and regional deans have been appointed by Forward in Faith who looked for a consensus among the priests in the regions when selecting the deans. Their task is to be a focus for the members and exercise *episcope* among them. However, a Catholic understanding of faith and morals, and a catholic practice of sacramental life, depends upon a structure which is ecclesial, if not *ecclesia*. Are our national churches capable of being moved from their old monolithic structures to a new federal model in which the orthodox can live and proclaim the truth to the majority? My own view is that any State Church is essentially opportune and will accept what it has to accept. We should seek the consecration of Bishops who will be for us a focus of unity and guardians of the sacraments, and for them will be proclaimers of the truth and drivers away of error. The 'Flying Bishops' could suffice for a time but they cannot be a long term solution. Female Bishops would render their position impossible. By their present office they inevitably accept living on an equal basis with what they believe to be an error.

An Ecumenical Faith

The separation of national churches from the universal Church has led to churches which retain some marks of catholicity, and indeed claim to be Catholic, but find that their internal polemic always returns to the sixteenth century. Somehow they are ossified in a time capsule, grappling with contemporary problems and then returning to their foundation documents. It is not without significance that what are called foundation documents are in fact the instruments of separation from the rest of Christendom; they separated the reformed churches from the universal Church and from each other. Anglicanism, unlike Lutheranism, claims not to be a Confessional Church, yet in its handling of the Prayer Book, Ordinal and Articles it behaves as if it were a Confessional Church. The Oxford Movement dramatically changed Anglican self-perception by breaking out of the time capsule and rediscovering the Early Church and a sense of continuity. Though for earlier brief periods the Fathers had been of influence they had never really been allowed to permeate the whole Church. Richard Hooker, the formative Anglican theologian, writing in the first decades of separation made extensive use of the early Fathers but stopped at the fifth century leaving a thousand years as a kind of vacuum. However in 1836 Newman and Pusey began translating the Fathers into English. For them the consensus of the Fathers was the standard and measure of Christian Faith and practice. The impact was enormous. For the first time Anglicans saw themselves in relationship both to the Patristic Church and the great churches of East and West.

From the very outset the Tractarians saw that dis-establishment was not in itself the issue. What really mattered was the authority of the Church and how it was exercised. The ideas in Newman's Tract One are strangely relevant to the contemporary situation even if the language seems dated.

'Should the Government and Country so far forget their God as to cast off the Church, to deprive it of its temporal honors and substance, *on what* will you rest your claim of respect and attention which you make upon your flocks? Hitherto you have been upheld by your birth, your education, your wealth, your connexions; should these secular advantages cease, on what must CHRIST'S Ministers depend? Is not this a serious practical question? We know how miserable is the state of religious bodies not supported by the State. Look at the Dissenters on all sides of you, and you will see at once that their Ministers, depending simply upon the people, become the *creatures* of the people. Are you content that this should be your case? Alas! can a greater evil befall Christians, than for their teachers to be

guided by them, instead of guiding? How can we "hold fast
the form of sound words," and "keep that which is committed to our trust," if our influence is to depend simply on
our popularity? Is it not our very office to *oppose* the world,
can we then allow ourselves to *court* it? to preach smooth
things and prophesy deceits? to make the way of life easy to
the rich and indolent, and to bribe the humbler classes by
excitements and strong intoxicating doctrine? Surely it must
not be so; – and the question recurs, on *what* are we to rest
our authority, when the State deserts us?

'CHRIST has not left His Church without claim of its
own upon the attention of men. Surely not. Hard Master He
cannot be, to bid us oppose the world, yet give us no
credentials for so doing. There are some who rest their
divine mission on their own unsupported assertion; others,
who rest it upon their popularity; others, on their success;
and others, who rest it upon their temporal distinctions.
This last case has, perhaps, been too much our own; I fear
we have neglected the real ground on which our authority is
built, – OUR APOSTOLICAL DESCENT.

'A notion has gone abroad, that they can take away your
power. They think they have given and can take it away.
They think it lies in the Church property, and they know
that they have politically the power to confiscate that property. They have been deluded into a notion that present
palpable usefulness, produceable results, acceptableness to
your flocks, that these and such like are the tests of your
Divine commission. Enlighten them in this matter. Exalt
our Holy Fathers the Bishops, as the Representatives of the
Apostles, and the Angels of the Churches; and magnify
your office, as being ordained by them to take part in their
Ministry.'[1]

The Catholic Revival was to have an enormous influence upon
the development of the Church of England. However, the
trend in the last thirty years has been the rapid dissolution of
its principles and aims. Dr. Gareth Bennett in the Crockford
Preface puts the issue clearly.

'Even where theological scholars are priests or ministers
there is a tendency to bridge the gap between their work on

early Christianity and their participation in the present life of the Church by a downgrading of the value of Christian tradition. The most notable casualty has been the study of ecclesiastical history which appears now to have a low priority on the agenda of theological faculties. If Anglicans once did their theology through a study of the historical experience of the Christian community that seems no longer to be the case, and the notion is in eclipse that the spirituality or the teaching of the era from the Fathers to the Reformation has anything to offer the modern Church.... Clergy without a sense of there being some authority in the historic experience of the Church may well come to think that theology is the latest fashionable theory of theologians. It is now clear that this weakening of the distinctive character of Anglicanism is beginning to have its effect on the coherence of the Communion.'[2]

A true Ecumenical theology must have as its basis that which was the agreed basis of the whole Church before the Great Schism. This means at the very least the Seven Ecumenical Councils, and the writings of the Fathers, with a sense of continuity to the time of the Reformation. This is common ground between Rome and Orthodoxy and the common inheritance of all Christians. We must evaluate our confessional statements, and our particular history in the light of them, and not work the other way round. We are judged by history, we do not judge it.

It is only through the perspective of all Seven Ecumenical Councils that we arrive at an orthodox Christology. Peter Toon in his recent work[3] demonstrates that together they present us with the Christian tradition and apart they offer us the possibility of being misled. The true nature of Christ is not readily apparent to all readers of the Scriptures. Our perceptions need to be informed by the Conciliar Tradition. Orthodox Protestants often proclaim a conciliar faith without being at all aware where it comes from.

The picture presented by the authors of this book is one of the degradation of Christianity. However, there is an interesting counter-phenomenon taking place particularly in America. There Christians, mainly from non denominational Protestant churches, are finding themselves challenged, changed, and catholicised by reading the patristics and studying the Councils. Two movements are worth mentioning. The first is the 'Pilgrimage to Orthodoxy'. This started with fundamentalist leaders and members of the Campus Crusade for Christ who eventually found their way to the Antiochene Orthodox Church. One of their leaders explained what happened.

'So they asked themselves: What happened to the Church which Christ founded? For they preferred instead to send their converts to such a New Testament Church. The question is very basic. Is there a Church which today meets the criteria of Christ's Church?

'The group of campus evangelists decided to separate and research the question independently; at an appointed hour, they would then meet again to share their findings. When they met together to exchange their information, to their amazement they were all in agreement.

'They found that the Church of Christ, as described and depicted in the ancient documents pertaining to the life and practice of the early Church, was a Church that was Eucharistic, evangelical, and missionary. They also discovered that bishops were important figures in the life of this Church. The bishops represented Christ and the Apostles; they presided over the Eucharist, "teaching aright the word of truth" through a special *charisma veritatis* given to them. The bishops essentially guaranteed the unity of both the local and the universal catholic Church. Presiding over the *one* Eucharist of the *one* Church, the bishops' interdependence in communion with one another was the pattern of Christian unity and united Christian mission to the world given to the Church since apostolic times.

'In searching for this Church, they reviewed the history of Christendom and realised that at the time of the great councils (AD 325–787), the Truth was with the Church of these Councils.'[4]

A similar movement has taken place amongst independent Charismatic Churches who have been prompted to form the Charismatic Episcopal Church. Episcopal ministry, orthodox faith, and liturgical and sacramental worship have become the marks of this rapidly growing Church. They have been joined by some Episcopal Church (Anglican) parishes. Both these movements are momentous changes for non denominational Protestants. When people study the tradition they are prompted to change.

The churches of the reformation diaspora must seek to conform themselves to the common catholic heritage. Particularly this must be seen in the formation of the clergy. In recent decades the trend in England has been towards the ordination of those who had already started another career, and are often in middle life. Training has become shorter, and less academic, and more and more priests are trained in part-time courses. A Church which does not feel confident in selecting and training the young and unformed is a Church which has little self belief. The Church needs young men of integrity with intellectual ability, rather than second careerists who have completed their education. Faith must be the first demand. It is not unknown in England to find liberal clergy who do not attend Church on holiday, and in Scandinavia it is common-place to find clergy not worshipping when they are not on duty!

A return to rigorous intellectual formation within the tradition, alongside spiritual formation, is the only hope for the Church. Without it the clergy will become little more than hobbyists, believing social workers who are incapable of meeting the challenges of the modern world. The present situation with independent colleges forming their students in ways at variance with other colleges whose students will eventually serve in the same dioceses shows unbelievable theological levity. Practice and belief taught in one college will be attacked in another. The formation of a clergy who will be able to instruct the laity in the Tradition is the first major task facing the Church. In the present situation where there is a real shortage of priests anyone who sought to select candidates and prepare them outside the system, as Kelham and Mirfield did in a previous age, would win the day.

Anglicans and Lutherans also need to come to terms with the uncomfortable fact that it is only in the Documents of Vatican II that they find a consistent presentation of the Christian Faith addressed to the problems of the modern world. Recognisably an expression of authentic Christian faith, these documents have an authority far beyond those who concede authority simply on the basis of origin.

The other issue that needs to be faced is that of the Papacy. Orthodox and Anglican Christians accept the Bishop of Rome as the first bishop of Christendom. Many other Christians accept the office but oppose the way it is presently operated. Interestingly some other Christians who reject the office, and indeed episcopacy itself, recognise that the Pope consistently speaks for Christian values in an increasingly secular world. The issue of Primacy needs to be recognised, and if accepted, implemented.

An Ecumenical Ministry

The ministry has always been one of the hallmarks of the Church of Jesus Christ. The Church of England states in the ordinal that the threefold ministry dates from the Apostles' time. If this is an over-simplification there can be little doubt that the Ministry has always been held to be integral to the life of the Church and the threefold ministry very rapidly became normative. The Episcopal ministry is of particular importance because it is seen as an extension of the apostolic office and the focus of the life of the Church. Bishops are the focus of the life of the local Church, the teachers and pastors of the faithful, and are charged with driving away error. Collectively, meeting in council, they have always been the deciders of doctrinal matters. Luther appealed for an Ecumenical Council to resolve the crisis of the reformation. His appeal was not answered. Anglicans have often suggested a new council. Would Luther's successors, or Cranmer's, accept the findings, or the teachings, of such a council if it were ever called? Recent events suggest they would not. Much of the Anglican approach to the ancient churches is one of innate superiority. 'We know better' is the mark of a sectarian, not of a catholic Christian.

It needs to be asked whether Anglican and Lutheran Bishops would individually accept the teaching of a new Ecumenical Council. If not, they cannot in any real sense claim to be

Catholic bishops. If they could, some would need to be asked
why they presently operate, and teach, that which sits well
outside the universal Christian tradition. How can they uphold
and teach that which they know in their heart of hearts would
not be upheld by any such council?

Sacraments are sure and certain signs of the Kingdom and
instruments of God's grace. A serious problem for Anglicans
is that they believe that they have the ministry of the apostolic
Church. Orthodoxy has ignored this claim and Rome has
rejected it calling Anglican Orders 'absolutely null and utterly
void'. These are hard words and have always caused great
offence to Anglicans. We may disagree but they leave us with
a problem. If the majority of Christendom rejects our orders
in what sense are our sacraments sure and certain signs? We
may state that they are, we may passionately believe that they
are, but the question remains. This question is just as real for
Lutherans, many of whom are at this moment incorporating
Anglican succession into their own episcopacy in order to
quiet Anglican concerns. The concerns of individual churches
hardly seem to be the issue. If we know that an Episcopal
ministry with a tactile succession was an important and much
prized fact in the early Church, indeed a mark of its authen-
ticity, then we have to be certain that we possess it. The same
problem exists for Lutherans.

The Papal decree caused a great deal of unease in the
Church of England and in the 1920's some leading anglo-
catholics did their best to engineer the participation of Old
Catholic Bishops in Anglican ordinations. The early participa-
tions were accompanied by Latin certificates stating a catholic
intent. By now nearly all Anglican ordinations must contain
this strain. However it has not resolved the question. Indeed it
is difficult to see how it could. What is the nature of the
ministry in a church containing those who believe in a very
catholic view of the eucharistic sacrifice alongside those who
believe the eucharist is a bare memorial, or those who assert
Christ is objectively present alongside those who believe any
presence is purely subjective? What is the view of the Church
on this matter, and if it has a view why is it not universally
held? These contrasting views are not alternatives. If one is
true the other must patently be false, and a deception. They

can only co-exist if the Church either has no real doctrine or view of ministry, or is indifferent on the matter.

If the orders of Anglicans are invalid what, if any, is the significance of the participation of a Bishop whose orders are undoubtedly valid taking a secondary role in Anglican Consecrations? The issue is not at all clear, and indeed the question itself is painful for Anglicans. Surely it is time to seize the nettle and sort out the question. Assertion of apostolic faith must be alongside possession of apostolic order. We separate them at our peril. I am firmly convinced that this issue is one that affects our corporate psyche and disables our Church. Conditional Ordination by the Old Catholics, or others, would not demean us, rather it would clearly demonstrate that we are in earnest in the search for unity and truth. We would be firmly on a path of convergence. Certain signs need to be certain and anything that could possibly remove any doubt should be seized. Rather than asserting we would be sure!

Unity

There are two conflicting pressures at work in the modern churches of Northern Europe. One is corporatist, and establishment, and demands unity and conformity at any price. The other is local and ecumenical. In England parishes have been allowed to unite with other local Churches which the national church, or even the diocese, finds itself unable to unite with. A piece-meal patchwork quilt of local ecumenical experiments has been set up.

At the same time communion has effectively been impaired by the ordination of women to the priesthood. The Measure to ordain women recognised this would be the cost, and the consequent Act of Synod making provision for 'Flying Bishops' recognises that this is the case. Many Anglicans have left the Church of England to go into communion with Rome or Orthodoxy, and others have established continuing Anglican Churches. Many of those who have stayed have done so because these solutions which are offered do not have an ecclesial dimension which is true to their corporate history and life.

However a question remains, and will be heightened when women are ordained to the episcopate. Is the established Church capable of adopting a federal model, allowing a large group within it to do exactly what it allows some parishes to do? Are liberal Christians generous enough and charitable enough to allow those holding differing views on major issues of faith and order enough room to live with integrity? Furthermore, will they allow them to establish unity and Communion with a body outside the Church of England or the state Churches of Scandinavia? My belief is that the answer is 'yes' and orthodox Anglicans and Lutherans must work for that day. That they may be One.

Notes

1. J. H. Newman, *Thoughts on the Ministerial Commission respectfully addressed to the Clergy* (Tracts for the Times I, London, 1833).
2. *Crockfords Clerical Directory 1987/88* (Church House Publishing, London, 1987), p.64.
3. · Peter Toon, *Yesterday, Today and Forever* (Preservation Press, New Jersey, 1996).
4. Peter E. Gillquist, *Becoming Orthodox* (Conciliar Press, Ben Lomond, California, 1990), p.vii.

A Note on the Contributors

George Austin

George Austin has been Archdeacon of York since 1988. He was born in the old workhouse in Bury, Lancashire, in 1931, and after an undistinguished academic career he was ordained in 1955. He was elected by fair means to the General Synod in 1970 and ejected unceremoniously in 1995. As a Synod member, he was a Church Commissioner from 1978 to 1995, a member of the Crown Appointments Commission for three years, and a thorn in the flesh of the House of Bishops for the whole twenty five years. He has travelled extensively on church business to many parts of the world, and he has been involved in broadcasting, television and journalism for nearly forty years.

Goran Beijer

Goran Beijer has been Vicar of St Jacob's Church in the city of Stockholm since 1983. He was born on the island of Gotland in the Baltic Sea in 1940, and studied theology in Uppsala before being ordained in Visby in 1967. After serving as a priest in Visby he worked as Information Secretary for the Church of Sweden Mission in Uppsala. In 1982 he was sent to Beirut to work with the Middle East Council of Churches and to study the traditions of Eastern Christianity. He has been active in the Free Synod of the Church of Sweden since it began in 1983, and is synodical Dean for Stockholm. He is married and has two children.

John Broadhurst

John Broadhurst is the Suffragan Bishop of Fulham. He was born in 1942, and studied at Kings' College London (AKC and STh by thesis) and at St Boniface College, Warminster. He served as assistant curate in Bowes Park, parish priest in Wembley Park, and Team Rector in Wood Green, all in North London. He was a member of General Synod from 1972 to 1996, and has also been a member of the General Synod Standing Committee, and the Anglican Consultative Council, and has also been the Pro-Prolocutor of the Convocation of Canterbury. He has been the Chairman of Forward in Faith since 1992. He is married with four children, and his interests include gardening, history and travel.

Samuel Edwards

Samuel L. Edwards is Executive Director of the Episcopal Synod of America. A native of North Carolina, he is an honours graduate of Brevard College (North Carolina), The American University (Washington, D.C.) and Nashotah House (Wisconsin). A priest since 1980, he has served congregations in Fort Worth, Dallas, and other Texas communities. He has written extensively on behalf of traditional Anglican concerns and delivered the keynote speech at the first National Convention of Forward in Faith in 1994. He lives with his wife and two children in Fort Worth.

Roald Flemestad

Roald Flemestad was born in 1943. He is a Doctor of Theology of the University of Strasbourg and a senior lecturer teaching dogmatic theology at Det norske Diakonhjem in Oslo. He is regional Dean in the Free Synod and Chairman of the Norwegian Church Union.

Geoffrey Kirk

Geoffrey Kirk is the parish priest of St Stephen's Church, Lewisham, South London. He was born in 1945, and read English and Theology at Keble College Oxford, and also studied at St Chad's College Durham and the University of Newcastle. His doctoral thesis was on the Heroic Plays of John Dryden. He is the National Secretary of Forward in Faith. His interests include seventeenth century English Literature, nineteenth century art and architecture, and cooking.

Folke Olofsson

Folke Olofsson has been the Rector of Rasbo parish in Uppsala Archdiocese since 1980, and Docent (Senior Lecturer or Associate Professor) in theological and ideological studies at Uppsala University since 1982. He was born in Jönköping in 1943 and took the 'Teologie kandidatexamen' (B.D.) at Uppsala University 1968. He held a World Council of Churches scholarship for studies at Union Theological Seminary, New York, 1968-69. He became Master of Sacred Theology (S.T.M.) 1969 and Doctor of Theology (Uppsala University) in 1979, by doctoral dissertation *Christus Redemptor et Consummator: A Study in the Theology of B. F. Westcott*. He was ordained priest in the diocese of Skara and subsequently worked as a parish priest and chaplain. He has been Dean in the Free Synod of the Church of Sweden since 1983. He is married to Ann Sahlquist, physician, and is father of Johannes, Anna, Klara, Jakob and Gabriel.

Bernt Oftestad

Bernt T. Oftestad has been Professor of Church History at the Norwegian School of Theology since 1983. He was born in 1942 and became a Doctor of Theology in the University of Oslo in 1979. He was Chairman of 'Bible and Confession' 1979/80, and has been a member of the Executive of the 'Council on the Foundations of the Church' from 1993.

Dag Sandahl

Dag Sandahl was born in 1948. He has been the parish priest of Two Sisters Church in Kalmar, Sweden, since 1971. He is Rural Dean and Dean in the Free Synod. He is a member of the General Synod in the Church of Sweden, and of the Central Board and its Executive Committee. He is Doctor of Theology (Missiology and Ecumenical Theology) and Senior Lecturer at the University of Lund.

Stephen Trott

Stephen Trott was born in Cumberland in 1957. He studied Law at Birmingham Polytechnic before reading English at Hull University, and Theology at Fitzwilliam College, Cambridge, where he won the 1983 Cambridge University George Williams Prize for Liturgy. He trained for the priesthood at Westcott House, Cambridge, and was elected a Fellow of the Royal Society of Arts in 1986. He is a member of the Ecclesiastical Law Society. He was ordained in 1984, and after two curacies in Hull, has been since 1988 Rector of Pitsford with Boughton, in the Diocese of Peterborough. He has recently been elected to serve on the General Synod, where he has been appointed to the Legal Advisory Commission, and elected to the Legislative Committee.